# STRENGTHEN YOUR
# MEMORY

## A SELF IMPROVEMENT COURSE

# STRENGTHEN YOUR
# MEMORY

## A SELF IMPROVEMENT COURSE

### by Michael Fidlow

## foulsham
LONDON • NEW YORK • TORONTO • SYDNEY

# foulsham
Yeovil Road, Slough, Berkshire SL1 4JH.

ISBN 0-572-01609-3
Copyright © Bold Face Books Ltd. 1989
This edition © W. Foulsham & Co. Ltd., 1991

Printed in Great Britain by
St Edmundsbury Press
Bury St. Edmunds

# CONTENTS

# INTRODUCTION

CAN you remember a dozen instances in which you forgot something during the past week?

The answer to that question makes little difference, because you *have* been forgetting things—little things and big—and if your lapses have been forgotten, so much the worse. But, since you're reading this page right now, it's probable that your forgetfulness has been plaguing you more and more frequently. And you don't know what to do about it.

And you're asking me.

And *I'm* asking *you*: Have you tried to figure out *why* you've been forgetting? Have you noticed *when* you've failed to remember? Have you noticed *what* things you've forgotten?

Of course you *have* got a memory, and, unless I'm wrong, it's a pretty good one. If you wanted to take the time, you could sit down and rattle off literally thousands upon thousands of facts ... the "seven-times" table, who's Prime Minister of England, your middle name, if you have one, or, if not, that you haven't got a middle name, the formula for baby's breakfast, what causes hiccoughs, how to spell "hiccoughs", how to cure a rasher of bacon or a rash, how to obtain a writ of mandamus, how long it takes to boil an egg or get to London when the traffic's with you ... you've got enough facts in your mind to fill a hundred jumbo filing cabinets!

But for all that you still forgot to bring the car in to have the oil changed last week, your telephone bill sat in a drawer and went three weeks overdue, your secretary had to remind you that it was your wife's birthday, you put your report card down some-

7

where and then completely forgot where it was . . . and you're getting pretty discouraged over this whole memory situation. Well . . .

Remember this: Unless you *learn* something—really get it into your mind in the first place—you're not ever going to remember it! Unless you understand something the first time, the odds are that the next time will be just another first time.

Trace the thought back a step further, and consider this: Unless you *pay attention*, you probably will not learn. And another step—unless you're *interested, for one reason or another, you* won't be paying attention.

So you're not going to remember anything in which you don't take an interest upon first encounter.

Of course it's obvious that you must often rely upon your memory to bring you information about things which *don't* interest you. If you've been asked by the lady next door to pick up a quart of milk on your way home, maybe you don't care whether she drinks her coffee black or not; suppose you don't like your job, or school, or cleaning the house . . . these are responsiblities which you've got to meet. Even if you're not genuinely interested in some things, *you've got an interest in them*, right?

So: since the best way to remember things is to take an interest in them, and since you've sometimes got to remember things about things in which you're not ordinarily very interested . . . what's the answer? *Create an interest in them!*

—Ah, come on, how do you expect me to get interested in addressing two hundred envelopes, or putting out the *garbage*, or algebra!

Simpler than you think! *Get interested in exercising your memory muscles!* Make your memory your hobby, watch it work, teach it new tricks, carry it around with you and show it off, and pretty soon it'll be taking fine care of itself!

In the following chapters I'm going to suggest a few of the tricks that you can play with your memory, in order that many of the things you've been forgetting will become more fun to remember. At the same time, you'll begin to realize that some things aren't worth the time and effort it would take to commit them to memory, if they can be taken care of in some easier way; part of this book will be devoted to a number of memory-minimizers—suggestions for avoiding memory tasks which might cost a bit too much of your time.

It won't be a system, or a course, or just a book of puzzles to test your rote powers . . . but a discourse on the practical application of memory principles. And as you learn more about your own memory, you'll take a greater interest in it, and use it to better advantage. The results of all this will be evident almost immediately—in your daily life.

After a very short while, you'll start to get the hang of it yourself. And as you become more familiar with your memory you'll derive pleasure and satisfaction from the game of finding new ways to strengthen—and reinforce—your memory.

# SECTION ONE

*What your memory is . . . and what it's
used for*

*A little bit about what we mean by "memory"—the acts and facts
of remembering, both in your mind and "on paper"; and some of the
areas to be serviced by your memory's equipment.*

# 1

## THE GEM OF MEMORY HAS MANY FACETS

MEMORY is far and away the most remarkable of all your mental functions. Were your mind unable to store up an enormous part of all the information fed it by your senses, each new moment of existence would bring with it the necessity of "starting from scratch" in everything you think and do. You'd have to wear a little tag with your name on it, on the chance you might meet someone to whom you'd like to introduce yourself; every time you picked up a book you'd have to examine it to see how the pages turned . . . and you wouldn't be able to read it anyway, because the letters and words would be meaningless to you!

Everything you do is made easier for you by your memory . . . each activity is simpler because in the past you've had experiences which told your mind and body what to expect and how to act in certain situations. Your life is a continuous lesson, because the countless things you do prepare you for doing them again . . . because experience eliminates travel on the trial-and-error route by teaching you the right—or wrong—way.

Even if you were to leave your memory completely alone, without ever giving a thought to using it more efficiently, it would continue to serve you loyally and well . . . but, why settle for a meagre pension when, by investing just a bit of consideration, you can reap a vast fortune ? While attending a lecture you're sure to pick up a few tidbits of information, just in hearing the words.

But if you could know how to prepare all those facts for more efficient remembering, if you were able to multiply your chances of remembering the information, think of how much more knowledge you'd be able to absorb!

The first step toward strengthening your memory is to find out exactly *what it is*. There's much more to it than a bunch of assorted facts and ideas swimming around in the grey matter of your brain . . . as you'll discover when you read the next few pages.

## Your entire memory

It should be made clear, right about now, that in this book the term "memory" means more than merely the mind's retentive abilities: it means, to freely adapt the dictionary's assertion, *all means by which one can recall or make available to tongue-tip any information or knowledge one feels like using*. This will include every trick, gimmick and short cut that we can devise; anything we can do to avoid being caught in the mental cold.

Suppose we take a look now at your memory's total make-up . . . for our purposes, its parts can be classified into two basic categories: *"natural" memory*, or your own mind's function of remembering, and *"artificial" memory*—devices for retaining information outside the framework of your mind.

## All in the mind

Your natural memory is the result of an exceedingly intricate network of retention of facts, ideas and physical activity—all of which are learned through sensory perception, and then stored in your mind and limitlessly cross-referenced, for future use. This is how it happens:

## Facts

"Camembert just had six kittens." That sentence tells you, first of all, the fact that six kittens have begun to exist. It also reveals, in the word "just", the fact that their birth was quite recent. But, because of your mind's retention of other facts, previously learned, the sentence tells you even more—you know that Camembert is a cat, and that the kittens are her offspring, and that she is a lady cat. You know these things because of your previous knowledge that kittens—baby cats—are descended from female cats . . . information which comes from your mind's ability to register *facts*.

## Abstract ideas

Now, what is a cat? Can you picture one in your mind? Unless you know Camembert, your impression of "cat" will probably not be an accurate picture of Cam herself . . . but still, you have a very good idea of her basic parts, at least. This impression is the image of an *abstract idea*, one built on a whole slew of impressions in your past involving cats and cat-ness. Then, too, how many are "six"? One more than you have toes on a foot, three and three, one less than days in a week, half-a-dozen . . . another abstract idea that is so well documented in your mind that you need give the word—and the concept—no more thought than it takes you to think of what letter follows "G" in the alphabet.

## Motor activity

If you swim, or ride a bicycle, or climb up a little step-ladder to get things off a high shelf, or move your arm to avoid putting your hand into flame, or walk, I'm sure that you don't spend every active moment thinking about these things . . . they come to you so "naturally" that you don't even have to give them a thought. If you type, no doubt you can now type many more words in a minute than was the case the very first time you tried a typewriter. But that took time and practice. Through repeated experience, effort and practice, your mind comes to retain memory of *motor activity*.

But all this mental memory-activity is only a part of the total picture. Remember, our definition of memory plainly calls for *all* means of making information available.


## Your artificial memory

Even if you were going to be able to devote full time to the task of feeding your natural memory's supply of information, you couldn't possibly begin to nourish it nearly enough to satisfy your needs. When you come right down to it, you simply haven't got the time to remember all of the things you need to know every now and then! It doesn't pay to memorize the entire Edinburgh telephone directory on the chance that you'll one day have occasion to call someone there . . . when you need to, you can always look the number up! And when the time comes that you must call someone in Edinburgh *the directory becomes a device for reinforcing your natural memory*.

Few people can awaken themselves automatically each morning at specifically desired times, unless waking time remains constant (waking then becomes a habit, as long as retiring time is constant). But if you usually wake up at 8.00, and on one special morning you must rise at 7.00, you've got to rely upon outside assistance—an alarm clock. *This is a device*.

Suppose you have approximately 100 accounts in your sales territory, or 100 members in the club of which you're secretary, or 100 relatives and friends to whom you must send wedding invitations. If you've come to know them gradually, one or two at a time over a period of years, the odds are that you remember the addresses of most of them, or at least of those to whom you write most frequently. But what if you take over a new territory, what if you join a new club, what if you take on the task of sending invitations to the guests of the groom? You couldn't possibly expect to remember all those new names and addresses right off, and it really wouldn't pay to set yourself to the task of memorizing them at the first possible moment, for, to make their recall habitual would be quite a difficult and time-consuming undertaking. So you condense the task in a very simple way: you prepare your own little address book, writing in it the names and addresses that you need. When you no longer require the bundle of information which it contains, you can put it away; or, if the information is continually needed, you simply make a habit of carrying it with you, or keeping it convenient. *That book, too, is a device.*

Do you get the picture? First, your mind is able to feed your memory directly—ideas, facts and motor information (physical activity)—from its own storehouse of knowledge. Because your memory is serviced by the mind alone in such cases, we refer to this activity as your *natural memory*.

And when your mind is unable to furnish the information which you seek, you can aid your natural memory with external devices: your alarm clock is such a device, so are your address book, your shopping list, the dictionary, your wristwatch, timetables, cookbooks, the letters on the typewriter's keyboard whenever you have to look, ad infiniwhatchamacallit! All of this we call your *artificial memory*.

## Memory-minimizers

All sources of information—your own perceptions, books and newspapers, people, and in fact nearly every single thing with which you come in contact—can both supply information to your natural memory, and perform as artificial memory-minimizers. Why should you bother to memorize the population figures of Bechuanaland, when the almanac is right on your bookshelf? No need to memorize travel directions you'll need only once, when one of the passengers in your car can tell you what turns to make while you're driving there.

But when the information you want to make available is of so specialized a nature that no standard reference works or handy authorities are at your service, you'll want to contrive memory-minimizers that are precisely suited to your needs. For instance, the salesman's address book; the student's lecture notes and class schedule; the housewife's clippings of favourite recipes.

Later in this book there is a section containing a number of suggestions for convenient notes, charts and other devices for storing information which you deem sufficiently coverable by such measures.

## Memorize or minimize ?

Whether you're going to memorize a specific thing, or merely keep it available for easy reference by means of artificial devices, is of course up to you. Let frequency of use, importance, degree of actual interest, and so forth, guide you in deciding. But don't forget, it's very important that your external storehouse be accessible, and even in occasional command of your attention, lest you forget to remind yourself. No sense in preparing a valuable memory-minimizer, only to misplace it and its usefulness. If you use an appointment book, refer to it regularly, at regularly scheduled times; always keep reminder notes dealing with one subject in the same place.

By organizing your time to use your natural memory only for those things for which you require mental remembering, and taking care of the unnecessary-to-memorize in an efficient manner, you'll be able to cut your task in half with surprisingly little bother. By eliminating the chore of committing many little-needed things to mental memory, you leave your mind more free of interference, uncluttered and clear and with more time for all those other things that you'll want to have right with you at all times.

Having a better idea now of just what your memory is, you can proceed to the question of its practical application. In the next chapter you'll read about several uses to which your memory can and must be put, and while you're reading you can decide how best to tackle each specific area to suit your own particular purposes.

# 2

## HOW YOUR MEMORY HELPS YOU—
## A SAMPLING OF ITS USES

OF course you're quite concerned about your memory because of its occasional past failures, and you have a desire to strengthen it in order to avoid as many similar failures as possible in the future. This task won't be as difficult as it sounds . . . and for a logical reason: as you consider the areas in which your memory has operated, and will continue to operate, you're sure to discover that whenever you had to remember something that was pleasant you had little or no trouble; but when your memory subject was something in which you weren't very interested, you found the task more difficult! *Strong interest is accompanied by strong memory* . . . where memory is not-so-strong, it's safe to assume that interest could stand a bit of heightening—and that's just what you're going to do in order to strengthen your memory.

### Look for weakness

Here is a list, by no means complete, of areas in which your memory can come in handy . . . As you read through it, jot down in a notebook, or on a pad, the items to which you feel you ought to pay special attention when it comes to strengthening your own memory. In addition, jot down whatever else you can think of that you feel might be pertinent to your own particular needs.

WORDS

Spelling, meaning and use of words in both your own language and foreign tongues.

GROUPS OF WORDS

Facts that you'll need to pass the course, or sell the goods, or bake the cake; things you'll want to know when you discuss a book you've read or a show you've seen; speeches and other recitation, jokes, anecdotes and assorted quotations.

ARITHMETIC

Numbers to help you keep the budget balanced; current prices and values, to save you dollars and head-aches when the bills come in.

HOW TO DO THINGS

Instructions and rules in games, jobs and living, physical activities like typing, skiing, or dusting the blinds.

NAMES AND FACES

Remembering both of them, and putting the right name together with the right face.

PHONE NUMBERS AND ADDRESSES

Numbers which have an annoying tendency to get all mixed up in your mind!

WHERE YOU PUT THINGS

Being able to locate things that you've hidden "in a safe place".

CHORES AND APPOINTMENTS

Those things that, once forgotten, can rarely be rectified.

MUSICAL COMPOSITIONS

Both ways—being able to "name that tune", and being able to "tune that name".

KEEPING PROMISES

Avoiding the embarrassment and hard feelings which rise when you've failed to remember.

OBEYING THE LAW

Saving fines and avoiding summonses—did you renew your driver's licence; should you cross at the green . . . or in between?

WHAT'S DANGEROUS

The pot-hole in the road, the thin spot on the pond, the burning Autumn leaves, etc.

Now, think back. Have you been forgetting *appointments*? Perhaps you're not interested in the people with whom you've made them, or in the places you've planned to visit, or in the things you've planned to do.

*Names?* You've got to be interested in people, or, at least in learning their names for one reason or another, in order to be successful at remembering names.

*All about books* you've just finished reading? Perhaps your interest in the books hasn't been great enough to carry your memory beyond the moment when you read the last page.

*Promises?* If you really meant them when you made them, did you really *want* to make them . . . were you really interested enough to be paying attention to what you were promising?

*Where you put things?* What were you thinking about when you put them away . . . and when you tried to find them, how interested were you in what you planned to do when you found them?

## How great is your interest?

"Being interested"—*really* being in the proper frame of mind to pay close attention—can often be a somewhat confusing concept . . . sometimes you'll *think* you're interested in something about which you actually don't care at all; sometimes you'll be curious enough, but too sleepy to be really interested in what it is that you're doing; sometimes you'll be wide awake, and involved in something which would ordinarily interest you greatly, but there'll be too much else on your mind to permit proper concentration upon matters at hand.

Section Two of this book will examine the actual mental activity which accompanies remembering. You'll read about what the mind *does* when it is faced with a memory problem, so that you can better determine how to make use of its inherent characteristics.

# SECTION TWO

*What the mind does when it attempts to remember—the factors which make remembering easier and how to use those factors to aid in memorizing*

*You've already spent your entire lifetime developing mental habits . . . now here's how to use them to help you remember better.*

# 3

## YOUR MIND'S A QUIVER

YOUR life is touched by a never-ending barrage of sensory impressions—a continuous attack by countless little "sense-arrows", which invade your body through eyes and ears, mouth, nose and fingertips . . . all over you! These impressions crash the gates and head straight for your brain, there to be sorted and filed for future reference.

As you read this page, vision sensarrows are carrying its message to your brain; and because your mind is aware of your overall general goal, everything is being filed under the heading of "memory" . . . "making mine better". That, then, is your target: success at gathering information about the psychological aspects of memory, and utilizing it to strengthen your own ability to remember. Or, *turning the mind's own habits to your practical advantage.* Much like a matador studies the bull's style of charging and turning, and then uses this knowledge to help him turn in a better performance during the corrida.

### A helpful image

To better visualize several basic aspects of your memory's "style", try this: imagine your sensarrows to be solid things; some will be larger than others, thus less difficult to locate in your mental filing cabinet. Then, too, should several arrows bunch together, the resulting cluster would be much easier to find than a lone and lonely arrow.

Using this image as a starting-point, let's begin to analyze your mind's memory habits, and see if they don't afford a few suggestions for strengthening your ability to remember.

## Opening the drawer

Before those sensarrows can get into your mental filing cabinet, you've got to open the drawer. Let your sesame be the words, "I want to remember, I can remember, I shall remember!" As important as knowing the best ways to go about strengthening your retentive ability is your attitude. If you're convinced before you start that nothing's going to help, then you're absolutely right, even though you're dead wrong. The doubts that you have will always be present in your conscious thoughts, leaving no room for practical memories.

But *an optimistic outlook clears the rocks from the road at the outset!* If you're confident that you can reach your goal, the route will be fun, and everyone knows that fun is more fun than work! When you come to a hill, a difficult part of making your memory better, just making believe that it's fun will make it a lot easier!

Experiments have demonstrated that people generally retain memory of pleasant things more accurately, and for a longer time, than memory of unhappiness. So it follows, doesn't it, that by being an optimist to begin with, your memory is automatically a great deal better?

## The value of attention

Suppose you're sitting in your lounge playing draughts, and in the next room the radio's on and a news commentator is speaking in a resonant voice about

the latest U.S. satellite attempts;
a flood in Brazil;
a Lithuanian poet who won the Nobel Prize;
the day's cricket-game;
newest developments in women's fashions;
stock market activity;
the weather forecast.

From time to time something which the commentator says will cause you to perk up your ears and listen more carefully, because he's speaking about a subject which interests you. If you're fashion-conscious, you'll certainly want to hear about the clothes you'll be wearing next season. If you're a cricket fan, you'll be listening when he announces the scores of the games. If you've planned a fishing trip for the next day, you'll be curious about what the weather's going to be like.

And the news items to which you pay closer attention will make deeper impressions upon your memory. Do you know who won the county championship last year? Who won the Nobel Prize? What was the high close of I.C.I. stock last December?

*Well-attended impressions are large sensarrows* . . . they can be more easily located in your memory . . . *are easier to remember.*

## Motivation for paying attention

What are the conditions which enable you, or force you, to give your attention to one thing, and not to another . . . at one time, and not at another?

It has already been stated that a vital part of paying attention is *interest*. Now, the interest that I'm talking about doesn't necessarily have to be that genuine desire to know more about whatever it is you're trying to concentrate on, for its own sake; but, speaking in broadest terms, it refers to your *motivation*—any reason which you have for knowing or remembering.

And every reason that you could possibly have is one either of *reward*, or *avoidance of punishment*. Actually, both are pretty much the same: reward is a profit, while avoidance of punishment is a zero—better than a minus.

If you're genuinely curious about something, you desire to reward yourself with additional information about it. If you stand to make money by remembering more about the things you're selling, cash is your reward motive. If you want people to think highly of you for being able to intelligently discuss current events, or popular novels, or history, or anything . . . if you want people to think more of you for your remembering their names, or playing chess well, or reciting poetry, or telling funny stories, social acceptance is the reward you seek.

If you want to avoid the discomfort of having flunked your geometry course, or the displeasure of having forgotten to keep a promise, or the annoyance over having forgotten the main theme of the third movement of the Symphonie Fantastique, your reward will be the maintenance of security . . . avoidance of self- or social dissatisfaction. You are trying to avoid jeopardizing your chances of winning the reward of social acceptance.

Generally, *the stronger your motive for remembering something, the greater an interest you'll take in it, and, consequently, the greater your attention will be*. And, when you pay attention, you stand a better chance of remembering!

Now . . . precisely what are the circumstances which act as motivations for remembering, and how do they do it?

## Impulsive curiosity

Impulsive curiosity is that trait which induces you to take a second look, or to try to find out more about something, because you can't quite believe what you saw or heard the first time. The *surprise*, the *exaggeration*, the *intense*, the *unusual* . . . these things provide vivid impressions—large sensarrows. Someone swims across the English Channel. A woman's hat contains a live bird in a cage. A new species of animal is discovered. You meet a man who's nine feet tall. You smell garlic for the first time. You see a building constructed entirely of glass.

## Curiosity out of familiarity

Curiosity inspires you to want to know more about something, after a little information, or even a lot, has aroused your genuine interest. Your hobby, your country, celebrities, a member of your family, something about which you don't fully understand, and would like to . . . these things, and countless others like them play familiar roles in your everyday life. When someone begins to speak about something and you recognize what it is he's speaking about, your personal pride and ego will focus your attention upon it, so that you might learn even more about it.

## Competitive nature

Man instinctively likes to *win*—arguments, athletic contests, fights, games . . . his ego is satisfied when, after pitting his mind, or his body, or both, against other men, nature, or his own past performances, he comes in first. If you bring yourself to believe that you might become an excellent card player, your chances of remembering the rules and the finer points of play increase tremendously, because your motive is inborn, and your goal appears close enough to induce you to reach out for it. If you won a spelling bee in the fifth form, chances are that you'll forever take pride in your superiority at spelling, and consequently will remember how to spell difficult words with comparative ease. All this ties in with ego, and desire for social approval.

## Money, fame, possessions

The cash profit is a powerful motivation indeed. The contestant
on a quiz show will show an amazing command of knowledge
about the subject which can win for him security, the luxuries he
has always sought, the fulfilment that comes of being revered by
many people. The commission incentive endows salesmen with
the drive to remember enormous gobs of information, from
names of customers to the smallest factual details about products.

And so forth . . . motivation, based on desire for reward or
fear of loss, inspires attentiveness, which in turn produces strong
memories. When you open the filing cabinet drawer, when you
prepare your mind to receive information, the sensarrows come
pouring in from whatever direction your sights are focused on.

Once you have directed your interests, factors involving the
nature of the sensarrows, in regard to their relation to other
sensarrows, come into play. . . .

## Association

When an impression reminds you of other past impressions, it
hangs in your conscious observation for just a little tiny bit longer,
and then becomes a stronger memory. Suppose you see a picture
of the flag of Iran. You might notice at the time that its colours
are the same as the colours of the Italian flag, which you remember
because some Italian friends always dress up the house for
Christmas in red and green. Or, maybe those colours are in your
curtains. Or perhaps as a painter or printer your work involves
colours, and you're reminded by the Iranian flag that red and
green can be mixed to produce a deep brown. Or maybe your
name is George W. Randall, and your initials tell the colours,
top to bottom—green, white, red.

Remember, your mind is elaborately cross-referenced . . . and
any sensory impression is just as likely to touch off a reminiscence

of something seemingly unrelated, as one of something which is closely allied. And with every association the memory of an impression is reinforced that much more. One may conclude from this, therefore, that *the more you know, the easier it becomes to remember*.

Association is the fundamental principle behind every artificial "system" for strengthening memory. Here, very briefly, is how it works: By constructing your own list of things with which to associate, you can remember any other things that come along, simply by connecting the thing to be remembered with the appropriate thing from your artificial list. Then, by mentally thumbing through your list, you will be reminded of the thing you're trying to remember when you come to its partner. More about this very important part of memory improvement later.


## Pattern

Your mind tends to organize the impressions it receives, and to reduce them to simple formulas wherever possible. This saves it, and you, a lot of trouble, because the knowledge that something fits into a certain pattern gives you a head-start in trying to remember it.

The Arabic numeral system, which is the one we commonly use, is actually little more than an ever-continuing repetition of ten digits—0, 1, 2, 3, 4, 5, 6, 7, 8, and 9—in a never-changing order. Perhaps you've never counted as high as 355,966 . . . but you know as well as I do that the number which follows it is 355,967. That's because you know that seven follows six, in the system's repeating and repeating pattern.

How does this tendency towards pattern act upon your ability to remember? Well, for one thing, rhyming lines of poetry are more easily memorized than are sentences of prose. Words are easier to memorize than nonsense syllables. Sentences are easier to memorize than groups of unrelated words. Try naming all the letters of the alphabet, stating them at random without relying on the order in which you've learned them!

Furthermore, you'll find that it's easier to remember things in groups than singly, and less difficult to memorize lists when they are placed in alphabetical order, or in size place, or chronologically, or in any established pattern that will lend itself to your list.

## Sensarrow clusters

Remember those clusters of sensarrows that are so much easier to locate in your memory than lone impressions? We've already mentioned one way in which they're formed—association. The more you know about a subject, the easier it is to recall specific things about it, because each specific thing is hooked up to other sensarrows.

*Pattern* also plays an important part in this means of remembering by association: visualize your total knowledge of a subject as a sort of jigsaw puzzle, and think of each isolated bit of information about it as one of the parts. When you receive an impression from that part, you recognize it as part of the entire picture, and associate it with the overall subject, while at the same time classifying it in the pattern which is formed.

## More than one sense

Now we come to still another method by which your mind brings into existence those easy-to-locate sensarrow clusters. When you see an apple, a little vision sensarrow is discharged to your brain. When you smell the apple, an olfactory sensarrow shoots out at your nose. When you pick up the apple and take a bite out of it, touch and taste sensarrows join the others in your brain. Even the sound of the crunch as you bite down on the apple produces another impression by which you can identify the apple you're eating. So appleness can be identified by the sum of all the impressions which you've received: a round, red, shiny thing that smells and tastes such-and-such a way, and makes a crunching sound when you bite it. The entire experience leaves a much more vivid impression with you than would just a look at an apple!

## Repetition

Here's another supposition to suppose: You've found a brand new way to travel to school, or to work, or to the market. All you've got to do is walk two streets east and catch a bus that you never even knew about, until the people next door told you. (When they mentioned it, you paid attention because you were motivated by a desire to discover a better way to get where you're going.)

You walk the two streets east the next chance you get, wait at the corner for the bus, and discover that it is indeed a very nice way to get to where you're going. You decide that you'll travel that way from now on. So, each day you walk those two streets and take that bus.

The first time you take the walk, you look around you and notice the houses, the trees, the store windows, the sidewalks, and everything else. But you don't really remember most of it. The next time you make the trip the same sensarrows as last time pop out at you. And the next time, and the next time, and the next time. Pretty soon, you know everything about that route "by heart", and all because you've been exposed to it over and over. The sensarrow which you received yesterday from the elm tree in front of the third house from the corner has piled itself on top of the sensarrow which you got from the same thing the day before, and the day before that. *Repetition of the same impression anchors the impression firmly in your memory.*

This is the principle of memory which helps you to learn by

studying. When you want to make sure you can understand something and remember it well, you repeat it to yourself, again and again. Of course the number of repetitions necessary to commit the thing to memory will vary with variations in all the other elements that determine the size of the sensarrows. After all, if the sensarrows are fairly large, it takes comparatively few of them to build a visible cluster!

## Overlearning

You can, by studying a thing for a certain amount of time, commit it to memory well enough so that you can recite it backwards and forwards, inside-out and upside-down . . . well enough so that you really know it quite well—and still forget it a day later. This is because your retention "runs out of gas"—you haven't *overlearned*. Overlearning imparts longevity to your memories far and away out of proportion to the degree to which you practice it. As soon as you're sure you've got it, it's good practice to put in another half-hour on it, to increase the life of your memory by weeks, months, years!

## Interference

Just as a radio programme comes through to you better when no static disturbs your radio's reception . . . just as you can hear the music better when there's no dust on the gramophone needle . . . just as the contents of a speech are better understood when there aren't any boisterous hecklers distracting your attention . . . so your mind retains its memories more effectively in the absence of other activity on the same wave-length.

Consider these alternate situations:

A.　You begin at 1.00 o'clock in the afternoon to memorize a bunch of facts about the Revolutionary Period in English History. By 3.30 you decide that you have the material pretty well learned, so you hop off to the movies. After four hours of the American Civil War and the Indian Fights of the West, you return to your room to refresh your previous learning. But all that stuff about the West, and those Civil War dates and data have somehow confused your memory with Cromwell, Charles I and the battle of Sedgemoor. Before you're through re-learning the Revolutionary Period you spend another two hours.

B.   At 1.00 you get down to studying the Revolutionary Period and decide at 3.30 that you know your stuff. Then, for a change-of-pace, you go outside and play football. While you're standing around keeping goal your mind reviews what it's just learned, and there aren't any new facts and dates to confuse you. So when you return to your room to review, you find that just about twenty minutes of study are sufficient.

*Interference by material which is in any way similar to the things you've memorized, confuses your memories.* After a session with the roster of your customers, visit old friends, rather than going to a party full of strangers. After memorizing your speech for the PTA, bake a cake instead of reading that book you've been saving. This principle is an important one to keep in mind when you read about *spaced learning*—combining study with "strategic" rest periods.

## When forgetting occurs

It's a funny thing . . . *you forget the greatest part of the material which you are going to forget, very shortly after you've learned it.* The graph of your memory curve takes a sharp downward turn almost the second you stop memorizing, then gradually levels off as time goes by. Suppose you memorize 100 words of a foreign language vocabulary list today. Depending on how well you've done your work, you might remember anywhere from none to all of it, tomorrow. But, assuming that you've done a pretty fair job, let's say that tomorrow you still retain memory of fifty words.

On the next day, you might remember forty, then 35, then down to thirty words, which you'll remember for quite some time.

Now, if tomorrow you re-study the fifty words you've forgotten, by the next day you might know about 70 of the original 100. And if you then study the 30 you've forgotten, you'll bring your knowledge of the vocabulary up to a pretty high level.

The important thing to remember is that *the sooner you can review something you've memorized, the better off you'll be*, since your memory from original study will be fresher, and therefore much fuller. Perhaps this is why spaced learning—the next factor we'll discuss—is so effective . . . it provides a deterrent to rapid memory fade-out.

## Spaced learning

If you spend an hour at study, then fifteen minutes at a "break", another hour at your work, another break, and another hour of study, you will have learned more, and memory of the learning will last longer, than if you spend three—or even four—straight hours at work.

Perhaps this is due to the reverie in which you are bound to indulge during the break period, reasoning out in your own thoughts the things you've been memorizing. Or, perhaps your mind simply begins to wander when you press it for too long periods of time. At any rate, spaced learning really does work . . . try it. *Studying for several short periods of time, with intervals of relaxation, generally produces longer-lasting memories than does one long, intensified study period.*

## Fringe benefits of spaced learning

A peculiar trick which your mind occasionally plays is *remembering more of something some time after memorizing it, than very shortly after completion of the memory task*. This seems to be a direct contradiction of the memory curve, but it's a very specialized case. Soon after you've completed a turn at the books, you'll be able to remember a certain portion of the material you've covered, right? But, a few hours, or a day later, when you've spent a little time thinking about the subject, a few points which might have slipped your immediate memory will come to your attention through pattern and association with the related points which you have been able to remember. So, in effect, you are remembering a little bit more than you actually learned *at the time of study*. This phenomenon might be a delayed memory of the "forgotten" material's actual position on the page, or a belated understanding of the words which at first you failed to understand, but later found rational in the light of your thinking about the entire subject.

## Dredging for lost memory

Often a name you've forgotten, or a fact that you tried to remember but couldn't, can be brought into your memory's focus through reverie . . . think *around* the thing you've forgotten—remind yourself of every point you can which may bear an association with it. *It's easier to remember things that are meaningful to you, through their relation to other things you know.*

## Imagination

When you remember the name of a friend, or the appearance of a house, or the colour of a flower, you are utilizing your memory of past impressions. But when you think of your friend growing flowers in front of a particular house, despite the fact that he doesn't even live there, and despite the fact that you've never known him to be interested in gardening . . . you're employing your imagination. This is *active* use of the memories which you have *passively* collected.

Sometimes your imagination plays tricks on you, however. Have you ever walked into a room and gotten the powerful impression that you had been there before? I'm sure that you've experienced this "false memory" at one time or another . . . you can't help feeling that you've heard a song before, you're sure you know that face, why can't you remember when it was that you spoke about that subject in the past? Well, it's quite likely that you never did do any of those things, although you might have heard a similar tune, or discussed something related. Sometimes an impression will touch off a great number of isolated associations in your mind, creating the composite image of the new impression so vividly that you can't help wondering . . . But don't worry about it—it happens to everyone. Just try hard to avoid confusion between false and real memories.

Your mind's got quite a "personality", hasn't it? And now that you know it a little better, you're ready to analyze what you've learned about it in the light of strengthening your memory, and see what possibilities you've uncovered for turning its ways to your advantage. That's what Chapter Four's all about.

# 4

## CONSTRUCTING A FORMULA FOR IMPROVED NATURAL MEMORY

Do you remember the matador in the last chapter, and his practice of studying the bull's style of charging, turning, thrusting of horns? After he has completed the job of learning the specific characteristics of his bull, he plans the strategy which he feels will be most effective in using the bull's habits to enable him to win the fight.

In Chapter Three you learned about the equivalent characteristics of your natural memory—that is, you learned that your mind receives impressions through all of your senses, that it remembers better through attention, repetition, formation of patterns and associations, and so forth. And now you are faced with the task of determining how to go about using these mental traits to best advantage in remembering.

Your mind has *automatically* used its inherent traits for strengthening your memory, ever since you began thinking. Since your mind is, after all, your servant, there's absolutely no reason you shouldn't be able to *make* it do for you, whenever you want it to, what it's been doing for you by itself.

### Adopting an optimistic attitude

So . . . how about it? Have you proven satisfactorily to yourself that your own memory is potentially excellent? Will you believe

41

me when I tell you that you do have, within the framework of your mind, the ability to increase your powers of retention tenfold? As soon as you convince yourself that you *can* do it, as soon as you change that dubious "if" to a confident "when", your anxiety will disappear, and things will be an awful lot easier for you.

You learned that *interference*—other thoughts coming into your mind to crowd out pertinent memories—can greatly reduce yo ir ability to remember. The anxiety which you should have shed in the last paragraph was a form of interference. While you wondered about your intelligence, about how well you'll be able to remember, your thoughts were occupied by the *function of remembering*, and not on the things which you were trying to retain.

From that statement you can deduce that constant attention to "how well I'm doing"—constant worry about your progress—will only slow you down. Don't try your hardest to *make* it happen . . . *let* it happen! It will.

But . . . I have also spoken to you about the benefit of making your memory your hobby—watching it grow and teaching it how to serve you best. These thoughts do not contradict one another, the one telling you to ignore your memory, the other telling you to concentrate on it. Rather, I mean to advise you that it's good to know that you *can* successfully remember . . . bad to defeat your memory by constantly worrying about it.

To take care of this memory-is-superior-with-optimism trait, do this: *Convince yourself that you can do what you set out to do!* Compare it to the countless things you already have done with your mind—being able to recognize at a note or two every current hit record in the juke-box, knowing the proper aperture and shutter speed for every one of many, many photographic lighting situations, having the ability to whip up any one of hundreds of tasty menus, knowing by name every street in your neighbourhood. With each specific memory problem, show yourself beforehand that it's not too much for you to handle.

## Checking your work periodically

While you're in the process of working on each memory task, keep tabs on yourself by periodically evaluating your progress. Check yourself every once in a while, with an eye on your final goal, and without worrying about how well, or how poorly you're doing. Progress checks are good, in that they tell you when you've completed a task in memory, but they must never be allowed to interfere with the memory work itself, else they defeat their own purpose.

It should be simple for you to devise little examinations with which you can test your progress. Set up a definite schedule for taking these tests, and follow it faithfully.

## Bringing yourself to pay attention

Your attention must at all costs be present whenever memory is desired. When you have a natural interest—out of curiosity, familiarity, ego involvement—the task of finding a reason for paying attention is already completed for you.

It is, nevertheless, desirable to think consciously about your motivation when a memory problem comes along. Say to yourself, upon making a new acquaintance, "I must remember his name, because he, too, collects stamps, and I'd like very much to get together with him some time to discuss my own collection with him."

When natural interest in a thing is lacking, it then becomes necessary to search more carefully for a very good reason for you to pay attention. Ask yourself how you can possibly benefit by knowing this thing, or how you might suffer from your not remembering it. An awareness of your reasons for remembering something will make the work of memorizing it a directed task—something to do for a tangible profit.

And add to whatever motivation you decide upon, the desire to give your memory exercise! Analyze, upon completing each memory task, the mental traits which you used to successfully remember, and the ways in which you used them. This will give you greater insight into the means of tackling the next memory problem, as well as a deeper, more complex motivation.

### Establishing a goal

Every memory problem is easier to carry through when you let yourself know beforehand exactly what it is that you're trying to do. By concretely outlining the task, you establish a pattern for your memory to complete. You thus enable your mind to organize all of the material for memory in the light of the total subject, and everything you already know about it. Association is made easier, and you're bound to do a better job of remembering.

Say to yourself, "I must commit to memory every fact that I can about child care." Then, as you permit your mind to ramble over the subject, all the things you've read or heard in the past about child care will begin to come to mind. Each new fact that you learn about preparing formulas, changing diapers, nursing, and so forth, will have a place in your child care outline, and relate to other things you know about the subject. By establishing a goal for your memory, you have prepared a curriculum, afforded yourself a slide rule for measuring your progress, and brought to mind previous information about your subject. A tidy profit.

### Using all your senses

You learned in Chapter Three that deeper, longer-lasting memories will be produced through the practice of opening as many doors as possible to the information which you want to receive. The impressions which you receive through sight add to those which strike your ears; the "feel" of something strengthens the memory which its taste has given you.

This trait comes in very handy when you are put to the task of memorizing [verbatim] speeches, poems, and the like. Reading the material aloud will produce the sounds, as well as the sight of the words, making your impression doubly strong. It also creates the visual image of the use to which you will have to put your learning. And when you have completed your memorizing work, or partially completed it, recitation serves also as a progress check.

## Utilizing the technique of repetition

If repeating something, over and over, will enable you to remember it better, then, by all means, repeat it! The formula of remembering-through-repetition is a mental trait which you have always used . . . when your mother called you by name the fiftieth, sixtieth, five-hundredth time, you began to get the idea that "Philip" was definitely associated with your own presence —of absence. You learned your name through its repeated use whenever you were connected with something.

Remembering-through-repetition relates to spaced learning, avoidance of interference, review-to-prevent-forgetting, and over-learning. Upon undertaking to memorize something, set up a schedule of study and review, with a thought to the best possible ways of employing repetition. Think of reviewing your material before the bulk of forgetting has occurred—as soon as possible after your initial memorizing session. For an important memory task, plan to begin your studying in the evening, just before going to sleep. While you're sleeping, interference is at an absolute minimum, and review of the subject upon waking up will serve to repeat things that are still fresh in your mind. Of *course it would be useless to try to memorize something when you're too tired to concentrate.* If you want what you're learning to remain with you for a very long time, as close as possible to permanently, plan to resort to many more repetitions than are necessary to commit the material to memory superficially. Overlearn the material, through extra repetition.

## Applying pattern to your memory problems

Because things are easier to remember when they conveniently fall into established, or establishable order, the pattern formed by the facts and factors involved in a subject should be looked for at the outset, when tackling a memory problem. Since in many cases little or no pattern actually exists, it helps to construct one. In the memorization of a shopping list, should such a task become necessary, the only pattern that you'd be able to determine would be the actual number of items on the list. Knowing that you must buy ten things, and not eight, will at least tell you that your spree is not completed when you've bought eight. This pattern has a great value. But remembering the missing two items becomes less difficult only when they occupy unalterable positions in the pattern which you've constructed. If the list were arranged in alphabetical order, for instance, you'd be looking in your memory for items number nine and ten, both of which begin with letters later in the alphabet than "P" for potatoes, which was item number eight. Or, if the missing commodities were strawberries and cream, remembering one would probably give you the other, if you'd planned that they were to go together. And if they were mentally arranged to go together with the peaches which took up number seven, just before potatoes, you'd have no problem at all.

You form a pattern by which to remember things by grouping them logically, or alphabetizing, or placing them in any order that lends itself to the particular problem. Arrange them so that their initials spell out a word, or number them in size place, or visualize them in a meaningful group. Their pattern will give you additional assistance in remembering them.

## Breaking down big problems to little

Just as it's easier to remember "3/4" than it is to digest the same thing when it's written "63/84", long memory tasks are often better handled by breaking them down into smaller "bites". When a problem involves the memorization of a great many facts, or names, or figures, try to find a "least common denominator"—some means by which you can reduce the one enormous task down to several smaller, much less forbidding ones.

If you can find no convenient "least common denominator," then you should *arbitrarily* divide your task into smaller, handier problems. Try to make the divisions at points where you'll easily be able to tie the parts together through association . . . don't lose sight of the total picture, or you're likely to find yourself in a bind. Knowing the several stanzas of a poem is of comparatively little use, unless you can recite them in their proper order, so that they make sense as a total entity. And remember to remember how many parts must combine to constitute the whole, so that you may avoid the mistake of leaving something out. If you know that the poem you've memorized has seven stanzas, you won't think you've finished after having recited just five.

## Visualizing in your mind

If you want to remember to give something to someone, then picture that act in your mind. When you're attempting to commit a name to memory, picture in your mind the person whose name it is, introducing himself to you. When you want to avoid forgetting where you're putting something, picture in your mind the thing in its proper place, and yourself putting it there.

These little mental scenes will increase your ability to remember considerably. They serve to form an association between the person and the gift, between the name and the face, between the thing and the place you've put it. They each serve to establish a separate complete pattern—the donation, the social being, the hiding place.

## Looking for the unusual

Remember that unusual things—exaggerations, non-sequiturs, surprises—provide vivid impressions. You can utilize this trait of memory to help you remember, by constructing exaggerated associations, devising funny reminders, visualizing your subjects in ridiculous settings when studying them.

## Writing it out

The practice of actually writing out things that you want to remember serves a multiple purpose. It detains you at the thing for an extra moment or two, forcing your attention on it. It adds a sensory dimension to your impression of the thing, as does saying things aloud, by putting you through the activity of physically producing a reminder. It enables you to form a visual pattern of the memory task. All this serves to strengthen your impression of the thing, promising a deeper, longer-lasting memory.

## Providing an added incentive

Sometimes, in the tedious, time-consuming drudgery of the actual studying and memorizing, you'll lose sight of your reason for doing the work. When you've got a long way to go before completing your memory task, the reward at the end of the road seems a lot smaller than it really is . . . seems hazy, and out of focus. When this happens, you can supply your mind with an interim incentive—a sort of little reward for progressing part way.

Include in your study schedule a prize, such as a cup of coffee, or a piece of candy—to be awarded at the completion of a set amount of work. Not anything so wonderful that your mind is going to be distracted from the work at hand, but preferably something that you would only have taken time out for anyway. The big difference is that you'll be taking time out for it at the right time, when you convert the distraction into a reward.

Let's go back for a moment, now, and put all of these little things for facilitating memory together into a list:

1. *Adopt an optimistic attitude.* Prepare yourself for remembering, by letting yourself know at the outset that the task is within the limits of your ability.

2. *Check your progress periodically.* Set up a schedule for keeping tabs on your work, so that you'll know when you've completed the task.

3. *Establish your reason for paying attention.* Let yourself know why you're undertaking to learn, and remind yourself what your motivation is each time you falter.

4. *Establish a goal.* Know at the outset of the work just exactly what you are trying to do, so that you'll be able to tell yourself when you've done it.

5. *Use all your senses.* Get all the impression that you can, to help you know the subject better. Say things aloud, to get the added benefit of heard impressions.

6. *Repeat things.* Utilize the technique of repetition, as much as you deem necessary. When you think you've learned it, teach yourself a little bit more, so that you'll remember it longer.

7. *Look for a pattern.* Discover a total concept, within which you can organize all the facets of the thing you're trying to learn. Let everything have a place, so that you'll be able to know what's missing.

8. *Form digestible tasks out of large indigestible ones.* When the problem is a very long one, divide it into smaller tasks which you can more easily handle. With small tasks, try to group them with other things which will add depth to your subject.

9. *Let your mind see a picture.* Visualize—imagine things happening—as much and as often as you can, to form concrete impressions in your mind.

10. *Rely upon unusual images and associations.* Look for vivid ways of impressing memorizing problems on your mind.

11. *Write it out.* Make your impressions more vivid, by taking a little extra time to set them down on paper.

12. *Promise yourself extra rewards.* Provide your mind with additional incentives for getting the work done, in little things that you're going to get anyway. Convert distractions into profits.

These twelve pointers form a programme which, when followed, will provide your mind with a handy framework in which to exercise its memory muscles. They constitute a formula with which you'll be able to direct your mental efforts. And they let you stop along the way, to see how you're doing, and to watch your memory as it learns how to handle future tasks.

So now you have a simple, dozen-point formula for improving your natural memory. In the next section, you'll read first about some specific devices which utilize these pointers—memory tricks which will be of great assistance in turning your mind to practical use in certain situations; and then, you'll learn more about that other, equally important aspect of your memory—the artificial storehouse, with which you conveniently dispose of much of your memory work by means of artificial devices.

# SECTION THREE

*The practical application of principles which affect natural and artificial memory*

*A discussion of some of the systems and devices which utilize and exploit, for practical remembering, the built-in characteristics of your memory.*

# 5

## HOW TO STRENGTHEN YOUR
## NATURAL MEMORY

In the previous chapter you were introduced to a short list of basic principles of remembering, the use of which should enable your natural memory to work with a greater degree of efficiency. Boiled down into simple sentences, here's the list:

1. *Adopt an optimistic attitude.*
2. *Check your progress periodically.*
3. *Establish a reason for paying attention.*
4. *Establish a goal.*
5. *Use all of your senses.*
6. *Repeat things.*
7. *Look for—or construct—a pattern.*
8. *Break down large tasks into small, digestible ones.*
9. *Let your mind see a picture.*
10. *Rely upon unusual images and associations.*
11. *Write things out.*
12. *Promise yourself extra rewards.*

### A step ahead

Following these simple precepts in your pursuit of a better memory, just as they are here stated, will improve considerably your ability to remember things. But, by further using their elements in devised methods—combining their functions and values to produce systematic working plans, you'll find yourself able to establish definite programmes for memorizing—organized attacks upon the undesirable bugaboo of forgetfulness.

In the following pages, you'll find outlined several of these practical plans for memorizing efficiently and effectively. In each case the basic principles of remembering will play a vital part, both independently, and in combination with one another. But, just as is the case whenever short cuts are sought, hazards pop up with each little memory trick. You've got to know when and where to use methods of speeding up your memory processes, and their relative benefits and shortcomings.

## Association—in depth

A chartreuse automobile spins past you as you take a stroll, and you're reminded that you have to bring your chartreuse dress to the dry cleaners. Upon being introduced to a Mr. Gabriel Horn, you remember that you've been planning to bake an Angel-Food cake this week. A cute little piggy bank in a toy store window catches your eye, and you suddenly realize that you've got to send in the latest premium on your life insurance policy.

Such connections, unusual or otherwise, are manifestations of your mind at work. You receive sensory impressions, which touch off associations with memories of previous experiences, bringing into focus the reminders that you need.

And then there are those times that the reminder is a step away from the association—"middle-man" associations. . . . The chartreuse automobile reminds you of the party Saturday night at the Jones's, because at the time you received the invitation you thought that you might wear your chartreuse dress. When you first hear Mr. Horn's name you say to yourself, "That reminds me—it's Charlie's birthday next Friday." That's because you remember that Charlie likes Angel-Food cake. The cute little piggy bank reminds you of the appointment you have with the doctor at the beginning of next week, to see if your health will carry you to a ripe old age.

## Giving your associations direction

Your mind automatically associates new impressions with old memories—at any time, for any obscure reason, and to any degree. Meeting an old army buddy might, though an unconscious chain of several associations, remind you that you forgot to turn the water off this morning, or that there's a real bad movie playing at the theatre down the street, or that you shot a 93 on the golf course last Sunday. You experience something and think of something else, apparently unconnected, and your mind's doing all that for you . . . automatically!

Now, suppose you were to channel all of that mental associating power into specific directions, with very definite goals? It seems logical, doesn't it, that you should be able to pull off some very neat memory tricks . . . with just a little bit of well-directed effort!

Associations can be, and most often are, chance occurrences, like your connecting a thundershower with the tear in the top of your convertible . . . but of course there's no guarantee that you're going to see a bank in a toy store window just in time to remind you to write that cheque for the insurance company; it would be a pity if Charlie had to do without your delicious cake on his birthday, because you never met Mr. Horn; if by some chance you should see only black cars one day, would you then be content to show up at the party in a wrinkled chartreuse suit?

Then again, associations, and the settings for them, may be artificially devised in advance, and with the specific purpose of enabling you to remember to do the things you've got to do, say the things you want to say, or find the things you've put away. The clichéed, but nevertheless effective string around your finger, having expressly been tied there to remind you that you must catch the 5.28 train home tonight instead of the 5.42, will most assuredly remind you to do just that, so long as its purpose doesn't become confused in your mind with the purpose of yesterday's finger-string.


## Handles, natural and applied

To what practical purpose, then, can the valuable principle of associative memory be put ? Well, in general practice, its uses are absolutely limitless! If with everything you learn anew you endeavour to find as many associations with previous knowledge as possible, there are that many more handles with which to dredge it up out of your memory's reservoir:

You learn that Mildew Hafiloc's birthday falls on the eighth of May, every year! As soon as you've been told of this snappy bit of information, your alert mind immediately begins to run through its files to see what it can come up with. And, what do you know! —The eighth of May is Victory-in-Europe Day, Harry Truman's birthday, the earliest-ever-possible Mother's Day, and the opening words of a scary little short story by Maupassant! That should be enough to stick the date indelibly in your brain.

And if something new comes along with which you, alas, find it impossible to make natural associations, you can "middle-man", and thereby apply your own handles to the thing:

Suppose you don't know what day V.E. Day is, and suppose you never heard of Harry Truman or Maupassant, and you hate your mother. Then you've got to find some other way to remember Mildew's birthday. By converting "May" to "five", because it's the fifth month of the year, you then contend with "5/8", or "58". If that happens to be your height, you can associate Mildew's birthday with your height. Perhaps '58 is the year in which you had your accident, and then you need only think of Mildew as an accident. Or else you remember that your alma mater scored that many points against Kenyon in a Homecoming

Day football game. "Five" and "8" translate alphabetically into "Eh". Or, reverse the numbers, as they do in Europe, and think of "85" as one higher than a book by George Orwell.

It helps if you can tie in the subject with the association, as we did above in the case of Mildew and the accident, but usually even this isn't absolutely necessary. The point is, that at the time you received the new information your mind connected it with the associate facts which you devised, and from that time on, each association became a mirror in which is reflected the new idea.

## Bringing in other principles

To strengthen the bond between Mildew Hafiloc and "Mother's Day", you might visualize in your mind's eye a cute, cuddly little Mildew, nestled in his mama's arms. Or you might picture him raising a glass of wine in a birthday toast to Mr. Truman. These are images both humorous and unusual.

If it's *really* important that you remember the date of this person's birthday, you can reinforce the associations which you've created by repeating them to yourself, or aloud when you get the chance, or writing them down the next time you're alone. If you care to, or dare to, you might even mention them casually to Mildew himself, noting the reaction with which he receives them.

## Patterns in things

If you know when to get off your train because your station is the one after Stark Street . . .

If you never have to fumble through your pockets when the conductor comes along because you are in the habit of keeping the ticket in your hatband . . .

If you're never caught dressed incorrectly for the weather (well, hardly ever) because you always check the forecast just before you leave the house . . .

If you can find your way around the golf course the second time out . . .

. . . then you have already been deriving the benefits which pattern has to offer. A pattern tends to organize the subject matter of which it is composed, introduces direction and order to things.

There is the overall pattern which holds together a group of facts or ideas: the teams in a Football league for instance can be named more easily when you know that there are exactly twelve, because you can set a numerical goal, and know when you've finished; 684 follows 683 because four always follows three when things are in proper numerical order; to find a particular fact in a textbook, you'll first turn to the back pages, because that's where the index always is.

There is the internal pattern which enables you to remember an individual fact: the spelling of "Mississippi" is easier when you realize that after the "M", "i's" separate double letters; you can remember the telephone number of the electric company because AMPere 2345.

## A design on pattern

Just as with associations, your mind has all its life been able to take advantage of the existence of patterns in things, automatically. And, just as with associations, it's logical that by providing specially-created patterns where they have been absent, you put another weapon into your mind's theoretical hands.

## Available associate patterns

What's better imbedded in your mind than the proper order of the letters of the alphabet? Well, when the order of a list isn't too important, you might try placing the elements in alphabetical order. Perhaps you'll be able to associate certain things with "number one", "number two", "number three", and so forth.

When it becomes necessary for you to construct or supply a different associate list than numbers or the alphabet for a memorizing problem, make sure that you aren't simply doubling your work. Spending too much time on the commission to memory of your guide-list is no wiser than filling the tank of an automobile that won't run!

If you're a chemist, perhaps you'll be able to make some use of the atomic list and the names of the elements: hydrogen, helium, lithium, beryllium, and so on. Any list of things which you already know in its proper order is fair game.

## Pattern in rhythm and rhyme

> *Roses are red,*
> *Violets are blue,*
> *If you don't win the race*
> *You'll be turned into* —— *!*

Can you supply the missing word? If you thought of *glue*, you did it for two reasons—first, you had remembered the association between races and horses, and the one between horses and glue factories; second, you tried to think of a word that rhymes with "blue". If the jingle had begun

> *Roses are red,*
> *Daffodils yellow.* . . .

then you'd probably have found it more difficult to think of an appropriate word to fill in the blank. The rhyming element provided an additional clue to the missing word's identity.

With a little bit of imagination, you'll be able to construct rhymes to help you in remembering all kinds of special facts. For instance, to remember where your friend Bernie lives, think:

> *To Brighton I must take a journey,*
> *If I should like to visit Bernie.*

Who went into darkest Africa to find Dr. Livingston?

> *David Livingston, explorer manly,*
> *Got lost in the Congo, was found by Stanley.*

Neatness, and aesthetic value, don't count. You can even resort to blank verse, if you like, because rhyme alone gives some little strength to your memory . . . but fewer words rhyme with "blue", than merely have the same number of syllables.

## Spatial arrangement

Here's a memory trick which involves both the principles of pattern and visualization. While you're memorizing a group of things, a list of names or dates or points you plan to make in a speech —try to have a picture of your list's order, either actually in front of you, or in your mind. Memorizing things which number a dozen or less can be aided with the face of your watch, by visualizing point number one with the corresponding numeral on your dial, and so on all around the edge. Then, you can remind yourself by looking at your watch.

Or you might study the list, if it isn't very long, while walking through the rooms of your home, assigning each item to a different room or piece of furniture. Just be sure that whenever you use this device you proceed in the same order.

The spatial arrangement which you use may be no more than a simple geometrical design drawn on a scrap of paper—the three points of a triangle, a nest of boxes, the five corners of a star, etc. It pays to write things out in their designated cubicles, so that your memory of the way they looked will reinforce your recollection of the things themselves.

## Checking your progress

Shall we try a little experiment now, just to see how well you're coming along ? Let's find out how you might go about memorizing the list of principles at the beginning of this chapter.

First of all, look for a pattern: There are twelve items—an even dozen. That's easy enough to remember, and even easier when you tell yourself that it "dozen" seem like a very tough task. Hey . . . that's the first principle—*telling yourself that the job isn't any trouble at all !* (1. *Adopt an optimistic attitude.*)

So take out your watch and work your way around the dial. At number two, think of a cheque, and of the fact that most cheques require that the value be written *two* times—in words, and in numerals. With the word "cheque" tied in this way with number two, you'll recall that the second principle says, *Check your progress periodically*.

The third principle tells you to *decide why you want to pay attention. Three's an* easy one. *Th' reason !* The word "why" is spelled with three letters.

For four o'clock, let's try an unusual association. Think of a *four*-poster, and then convert it mentally into a *goal-post. Think* that'll do it ? (4. *Establish a goal.*) The fifth one's not hard at all: you've got *five senses.* (5. *Use all of your senses.*)

What's a *six*-shooter ? A *repeater*! (6. *Repeat things.*)

To remember what the seventh principle suggests, we'll use both itself and number eleven, its dice-table counterpart: take a pencil and a scrap of paper, and draw a pattern using only sevens. On the dice, the numbers form a pattern by making sure that opposite ends always add up to seven. The word *seven* contains a pattern of odd consonants, even vowels. (7. *Look for—or construct —a pattern.*)

When you sat down to *breakfast*, you *ate*, and then digested your food. (8. *Break down large tasks into small, digestible ones.*)

For principle number nine, visualize a picture of your mind's eye itself, wearing a monocle with a string hanging down to one side. This resembles a nine. Associate the number with a monocle, something which helps you to *see*. (9. *Let your mind see a picture*.)

For number ten, think of a very skinny man standing alongside his very fat wife. That's an unusual association, isn't it? And, if you push your imagination a little, they might begin to resemble the "one" and the "zero" in number *ten*. (10. *Rely upon unusual images and associations*.)

Number eleven was covered when we worked on number seven, but you can further reinforce it by thinking that when you *write out* "eleven", it forms a pattern of vowel-consonant-vowel-consonant, etc. (11. *Write things out*.) Number twelve is the end of the list, and at the end of the job you get a *reward*. Think also of a baker's dozen, which, legend has it, consists of *something extra*. (12. *Promise yourself extra rewards*).

Now, should you want to call to mind the entire list of principles, all you need do is look at your watch and run mentally through the numbers from one to twelve. With each number your mind will pick out the related point by association.

Like to try it yourself? Here's something to work on:

> *Thou shalt have no other gods before Me.*
> *Thou shalt not take the name of the Lord in vain.*
> *Remember the Sabbath day to keep it holy.*
> *Honour thy father and thy mother.*
> *Thou shalt not murder.*
> *Thou shalt not commit adultery.*
> *Thou shalt not steal.*
> *Thou shalt not bear false witness against thy neighbour.*
> *Thou shalt not covet thy neighbour's wife*
> *Thou shalt not covet thy neighbour's possessions.*

Read the list through once or twice, and then go through it one item at a time, constructing associative handles for each. Make sure that you understand what each thing means, so that you can easily recognize it through its associations.

When you come up against a list of things to remember which doesn't require a special order, you're allowed to change the order for convenience.

## A simple addition to your memory bank

Having at your command two ways, instead of one, to remember something, certainly can't do you any harm—here's a very simple and, once you've gotten the hang of it, a quick way to construct an extra handle for nearly every fact and idea that applies for membership in your mind.

It's a simple gimmick, involving letter-number translation, and can be utilized in a number of ways. When you want to remember words, you simply translate them, through a convenient code-key, into numbers. And then you may recall the words to mind either directly, or round-about, by means of the numbers it produced. Conversely, the numbers that you've got to remember may be translated into letters and words, and remembered through the bonus impression.

The translation code can be merely the simple alphabetical-numerical order: A-equals-1, B-equals-2, C-equals-3, etc., but the use of this key necessitates the too-complicated procedure of memorizing the numerical standards of 26 different letters; furthermore, it prohibits your bunching together of the derived digits—you might forget whether "1215322" was translated from "A-U-E-C-V," or from "L-O-C-B-B," and so forth.

So the logical alternative is to assign letter values to the digits, 1-2-3-4-5-6-7-8-9-0. In one system which has been in use for many years, the vowel-sounds A-E-I-O-U-Y and the aspirant "H" and "W" have been eliminated from the key, for reasons which will become clear as you learn more about the system. With the remaining eighteen letters, it becomes evident that ten distinctively different *sounds* can be produced. And, with only ten digits to take care of, a fine key naturally evolves. Here it is:

Digit: "*1*". The dental sounds of "*D*" and "*T*". Both of these letters, in the lower case, are written with *one* vertical stroke.

Digit: "*2*". The nasal sound of "*N*". This letter is written in the lower case with *two* vertical strokes.

Digit: "*3*". The humming sound of "*M*", written in the lower case with *three* down strokes.

Digit: "*4*". The purring "*R*" sound. Remember this one by noting that the *fourth* letter of the word "four" is an "*R*".

Digit: "*5*". The lazy sound of "*L*". Remember that this letter stands for the Roman numeral *fifty*—made up of a five and a zero.

Digit: "*6*". The soft sounds of "J", "SH", "DG", "soft G" and "soft CH". Associate "sweet *six*teen" and "SHugar".

Digit: "*7*". The hard sounds of "K", "Q", "QU", "NG", "hard C" and "hard G". Remember this one by noting that while number *six* stands for *soft* sounds, number *seven* stands for *hard* sounds.

Digit: "*8*". The windy sounds of "*V*" and "*F*". Think of the word "fate", which is derived from combining "*f*" and "*eight*".

Digit: "*9*". The choppy sounds of "*B*" and "*P*". In a mirror, the lower-case "*p*" roughly resembles a number "*9*".

Digit: "*0*". The sibilant sounds of "*S*", "soft *C*" and "*Z*". The last digit in the list is "*0*", and the alphabet's last letter is "*Z*".

1. d, t (th)
2. n
3. m
4. r
5. l
6. soft g, j (soft ch, dg, sh)
7. hard c, hard g, k, q (guttural ch, qu)
8. f, v (gh, ph)
9. b, p
0. soft c, s, z

(A double-letter which retains a pure single sound doesn't increase the number value. Thus, the "*tt*" in "matter" translates to number "*1*". The letter "*X*", which stands for a double sound —*k*-plus-*s*—would be translated to number "*70*".)

## Compounding your interests

How, then, will your memory benefit with the utilization of this translation code-key? Well, let's begin with the problem of remembering numbers:

The value of mathematical "pi", carried out to four decimals, is 3.1416. This number might be translated into MeTeR DaSH— and you can visualize a man in track clothes running as fast as he can around a pie, which measures a little bit more than a yard in circumference.

Suppose you have trouble remembering the weeknight and time of your favourite television programme, a situation comedy called

"Open House" which appears on the screen every Thursday evening at 7.30. Convert "Thursday" to "5", because it's the fifth night of the week, and then translate "5730" to "weLCoMeS". An association between the word and the programme shouldn't be very difficult at all.

William Shakespeare was born in 1564—THey'LL JeeR; the year of his death was 1616—TCH, TCH.

So the procedure for using the code-key for remembering numbers is this: translate the numbers' digits into the corresponding letters from the key, and form *associatable* words from the letters by inserting vowels wherever it's convenient. (This is one of the reasons for eliminating vowel sounds from the key.) Then, simply repeat the association to yourself. While the order of the numbers wasn't a recognizable pattern, the order of the letters can be seen in the words it forms. Thus both association and pattern help you to remember through translation.

Of course if you're going to use this system for memorizing a long list of historical dates, it's important that your code words don't get mixed up; so make sure that your associative images are well-anchored to the facts they signify. To be extra-careful, you should use this translation method only as a system for reinforcing your learning, which you should accomplish in the more conventional way of studying in order to understand it completely.

What about remembering words with the aid of the code-key for number-translation? The system becomes helpful principally with lists of words which lend themselves to the device of visual imagery, and involves the use of an additional "middle-man". Before it becomes a short-cut, you've got to take a little extra time to build yourself an auxiliary word-list—simple little words which translate to the numbers of the code, and which lend themselves readily to associations. The procedure from there is elementary—build associations between the words in your list and the key-words.

In order to call to mind the things you've memorized, you just run through the key-word list, bringing to the surface those associations which you've created between them and the subjects. But you've got to know the key-word list as well, or nearly as well, as you know the alphabet, and to accomplish that is an entire job in itself.

It's up to you to decide whether or not you can afford the extra time it will take for this memorizing work—whether you'll have sufficient use for such a list to make its memorization worth your while. It's a one-time job, which will be reinforced each time you utilize the system, but it's a job nevertheless.

And of course you continually run the risk of pulling out the wrong associations, if you use the list for too many very similar memory tasks. With just a little diligence, however, you should be able to avoid such problems. No need to worry about mistaking an association with a recipe ingredient, if you're trying to remember the name of a character from a novel.

The method of constructing your auxiliary list will go something like this:

Number 1. This translates to "T"—the word "hat" translates back to number one, and provides convenient imagery.

Number 2. This translates to "N"—"hen" lends itself to convenient imagery.

Number 3. This becomes "M", and you can use "home" or "ham" or "yam" for your association.

Continue through the numbers as high as you want to go, and then set yourself down to the task of memorizing the list. The job shouldn't be much too difficult if you're really convinced that it's worthwhile, because you'll be able to do it mentally—on the train, in your bath, or in bed just before falling asleep.

Here's a sample list of twenty key-words—the outside end of the list is limitless—which you might be satisfied to use just as it is, or change to fit in more readily with your own particular tendencies for association:

| | |
|---|---|
| 1. ha*t* | 11. *t*oa*d* |
| 2. he*n* | 12. *d*u*ne* |
| 3. *h*o*m*e | 13. *d*o*m*e |
| 4. *w*i*r*e | 14. *d*oo*r* |
| 5. ho*l*e | 15. *d*o*ll* |
| 6. wa*sh* | 16. *d*i*sh* |
| 7. *c*ow | 17. *t*a*ck* |
| 8. hi*v*e | 18. *th*ie*f* |
| 9. whi*p* | 19. *t*a*pe* |
| 10. *t*oe*s* | 20. *n*o*se* |

Once you've memorized a list such as this one, you'll be able to use it over and over again, just as if you were working with the alphabet . . . but your associations will be more vivid, because you're dealing in picture-words, rather than with mere letter-symbols.

### To the test

Now let's see how the list might help in enabling you to remember something. For an example, we'll concoct a hypothetical "Things-to-do-tomorrow" list—*Watch a special morning telly show; Call electrician about washing machine; Bring clothes to cleaner; Attend ban-the-bomb rally downtown; Have auto repaired; Buy meat; Pick up snapshots; Wash the dog.*

Here we go: Eight things to remember; in a special order, so that it's not necessary to run back and forth between home and the shopping district. The associations—

1. *Watch a special morning telly show.*

The first word on our code list is *hat*; associate this with the first item by visualizing a TV set wearing a big top hat.

2. *Call electrician about washing machine*.

The second key-word is *hen*; visualize a big fat hen, with an electric cord connecting it to the washing machine, and billows of suds pouring out the door.

3. *Bring clothes to cleaner*.

The third word is *home*; just picture a big stack of clothes, with tags all over them, sitting on the floor in your living-room.

4. *Attend ban-the-bomb rally downtown*.

The fourth word is *wire*; visualize a tightrope-walker's high wire stretched between two mushroom clouds, and men and women with posters walking back and forth along it.

5. *Have auto repaired*.

Five translates into *hole*; picture your auto, all battered and stuck in a hole on the road, with a mechanic in a tow truck working to get it out.

6. *Buy meat*.

The sixth key-word is *wash*; picture a big, beautiful cow, with dotted lines along its sides, taking a bath in a pond.

7. *Pick up snapshots*.

The seventh word is *cow*; now imagine yourself taking that cow's snapshot. Don't worry about confusing this with the previous chore, because you'll think of both at the same time and do both in order.

8. *Wash the dog*.

Number eight is *hive*; visualize your dog jumping up at a bee-hive in a tree, when suddenly the bees rush out and run the hose on him.

The system of memorizing through paired associates, aided by the use of a number-translated list of key-words, will help you to provide bonus impressions and additional handles for remembering long lists of facts and ideas. Even if you don't rely entirely upon this method, the extra associations which it provides will give you that much better a chance of remembering things, and so its use will be worth something, at least. Just don't lose sight of the fact that you won't be able to remember the things you want to, if you don't understand them well enough in the first place to be able to recall through understanding the associations which you construct.

## Dividing to conquer

You are better able to digest the food you eat when your intake is composed of little bites, and you'll be better able to remember the components of a large fund of information if you memorize the components themselves, rather than undertaking to force the total subject into your mind. Just don't lose sight of the overall pattern, which helps you to understand the total subject.

If you undertook to remember the names of the counties of England, you'd probably find it quite difficult to name them at random. And if you tried to memorize them in some devised order, the weight of numbers might tend to mix you up before you got very far through the entire list of forty. An easier way to go about the task would be to arrange the names of the counties alphabetically, and then recall them letter by letter, noting along the way the pattern which is formed by the number of counties for each letter:

No "A's"; three "B's"—Bedford, Berks, Bucks; four "C's"— Cambridge, Cheshire, Cornwall, Cumberland; four "D's", one "E", one "G", and so on. Break down the alphabet into groups of letters to provide convenient, fairly even numbers of counties in each group, note the approximate size of each bunch and how many bunches there are, and the natural order of the alphabet will help you to tie the groups together.

Likewise for learning poetry, speeches and other recitation, the task becomes less tedious when broken down into several more easily digestible sections. To help you to remember the sections in their proper order, and to facilitate your transition from section to section, *build an association chain of section-identifying words*. Consider the following:

> O Memory! celestial maid!
>> Who glean'st the flowerets cropp'd by time;
> And, suffering not a leaf to fade,
>> Preserv'st the blossoms of our prime;
> Bring, bring those moments to my mind
> When life was new and Lesbia kind.
>
> And bring that garland to my sight,
>> With which my favour'd crook she bound;
> And bring that wreath of roses bright,
>> Which then my festive temples crown'd;
> And to my raptured ear convey
> The gentle things she deign'd to say.
>
> And sketch with care the Muse's bower,
>> Where Isis rolls her silver tide;
> Nor yet omit one reed or flower
>> That shines on Cherwell's verdant side;
> If so thou mayst those hours prolong,
> When polish'd Lycon join'd my song.
>
> —ODE TO MEMORY (excerpt), William Shenstone

If you were to try to memorize all nine verses of this poem, chances are that the lines would soon start switching themselves around in your mind, and you'd become pretty confused. But the six lines which comprise one verse would be few enough for you to handle. So memorize the poem, verse by verse, and keep the sections in order by selecting a key word or phrase from each and building an association between it and the key word or phrase from the next.

To illustrate, look at the three verses quoted above. From the first verse, let's take the word "celestial". It's not repeated in the other verses, so it should distinctively identify only this section, and it should lend itself fairly well to associative imagery. Likewise, in the second verse, we can use the word "garland". From the third verse select the word "Muse". Note that all three words occur in the opening line of their respective verses. This makes it simpler to start the recitation rolling as soon as each verses identifying word is brought to mind through the association chain.

And now to link the verses together. Upon completion of reciting the first verse, "celestial" will bring to mind "garland" if you think of the image of a wreath of stars. And, as soon as you've finished reciting the second verse, let "garland" remind you of "Muse"—the key-word which identifies verse number three—by associating them through the mental image of a circle of flowers reposing within the Muse's bower.

In the same manner, the six ensuing verses will be brought to mind through the rest of your nine-word association chain, prepared at the time you studied the entire poem. Make sure that you follow the author's meaning from start to finish, so that the individual verses will have meaning to you in context with the whole, else the key-words will lose their effectiveness, and won't be right there when you start to look for them. Try to select words which are early in the verses, and which convey an essential part of their messages.

The point-by-point outline of a speech, lecture or other work of prose will provide you with an association chain which will guide you through its recitation. The key words and phrases

which you select need not actually appear in the work itself.
so long as they represent it accurately, and impart to you the
significance of their particular passages.

## Combining for strength

Sometimes the information contained in the realm of one subject
will add depth and dimension to the facts which you are trying
to remember about something else. In the curriculum of a foreign
language course, for instance, the study of a selection for reading
will reinforce your knowledge of the vocabulary. Studying them
together will improve your ability to grasp the meaning of both,
and would be a better way of learning than merely studying each,
independently.

While reading an historical novel set in Victorian England,
you might become interested enough in the period itself to want
to learn more about it. You can add immeasurably to your
enjoyment and perception of reading for pleasure by also reading
parts of a textbook which covers the history of the time. And the
insight which you gain while reading the novel will reinforce
your interest and understanding of the material which is covered
in the textbook. Remember, the more interested you are in something, the easier it is to learn, and the more you know about
something, the greater your interest will be.

## Efficiency pays off

Can you by this time, remember the names of the planets of our
solar system in their proper order . . . remember the contents of
your "Things to do tomorrow" list? If you've paid attention to
associative reminders . . . *it's all in your mind!*

Each of these mnemonic tricks and memorizing "systems" is
well-founded upon the natural tendencies and abilities of your
own mind—they take advantage of its preference for pattern,

association, and so forth, and capitalize on the existence of your own great mental potential, assisting your mind's more *efficient* performance.

Efficiency produces gratifying results in avoiding the need for memorizing, when desirable, as well as in the remembering processes themselves. In the next chapter you'll read about how an efficient approach to the use of memory-minimizers can enable you to save yourself work, time, annoyance, and often embarrassment, through the simple expedients of "artificial" memory.

# 6

## HOW TO STRENGTHEN YOUR
## ARTIFICIAL MEMORY

Now, don't go getting the wrong idea—this chapter isn't going to
clue you in to a foolproof system for avoiding forevermore the
bother of remembering with your mind; that "bother" is one for
which you've got lots and lots of uses, and you don't have to read
a book to know it.

However, every day of your life certain circumstances and
situations *do* pop up, bringing with them the need for you to have
available some information or other—information which can
be just as satisfactorily, and much more easily, "remembered"
through the use of memory-minimizers. It takes *time* to memorize
things, and you haven't got enough time—there aren't enough
hours in the day—to feed into your memory's natural storage bins
all the information of which you have need from time to time.

### The role of natural memory

Even with the most efficient methods of utilizing artificial memory,
natural remembering cannot be entirely eliminated from any
specific task. On the contrary, it plays a vital role in virtually every
memory problem you encounter.

In the first place, our earlier investigation of the mind has
resulted in the discovery of a number of facts which will have
considerable bearing upon the manner in which we'll approach the

subject of artificial memory. Many of the principles which we've found to have useful application to the problem of strengthening natural memory will be no less applicable to our present concern.

In the second place, in order for your artificial memory to be of any use at all, it must rely upon its natural counterpart for the spark which can ignite the fuel that starts it running. Of no use whatsoever is the note you wrote to yourself this morning to remind yourself to get your hair cut at lunchtime, and then left on your dresser at home, alongside the book which you were supposed to bring back to the library.

Artificial memory is truly a fine and useful tool, but unless the utilization of memory-minimizers is efficiently organized and backed up by a bit of natural memory, it can't possibly produce the most profitable results—can't provide all the benefits of which it is capable.

## Interplay

Think of your memory as a total entity, composed of resources for remembering both naturally and artificially—the one part both assisting and being assisted by the other. When you seek the service of your artificial memory, your mind tells you where to look if you want to know how to spell "Eschatology", your mental memory knows from past experience that you can find that information in a dictionary or encyclopedia, or from some friend who has a knack for spelling or a knowledge of theological doctrines. Conversely, you feed your natural memory's stockpile with information derived from the resources of your external information depot.

In the next pages you'll read about several ways of organizing your artificial memory for maximum efficiency, and about several sources of external information which are, or can be, made conveniently available.

## "Ready-made memory-minimizers"

External sources of information are all around you. If you can't remember someone's address or telephone number, you can find that information in the proper telephone directory. If you're interested in knowing the principal products of Israel's industries, you can find that information in an encyclopedia or the almanac. If you want to know the names of the Tudor Kings of England you can turn to a history textbook. If you'd like to know Jeffrey Stansbury's middle name, ask him.

The trick, occasionally, is in knowing where to look for a specific bit of information. You have most probably learned, through experience, how to locate what you need in the sources which are available in your own home. And when you seek information other than what's available at home, you can save time and exasperation by inquiring of your local librarian, or a friend who's likely to know.

## Using books

When looking for specific information in a particular book, the first thing to do is consult the index, if there is one, or the table of contents. Failing to satisfy your curiosity with either of these aids, you might get a pretty good idea of where to look within the book by poring over the introduction, and noting the overall pattern which the author plans to follow through the pages.

In your personal library, try to keep books on related subjects in roughly the same vicinity on the shelves. In this way, you'll know better where to find the book you're looking for, and not waste valuable time in unnecessary searching.

Don't be afraid to mark up the pages of your own books! They are intended for your use, and if underlining, writing in the margins or listing subjects and page numbers on the inside of the cover enables you to find information which you might want in the future, by all means do so!

## Relying on people

Information which is of a personal nature, that is, directly pertinent to an individual whom you know or with whom you can get an audience, is of course most reliably obtainable through the individual directly concerned. The telephone, or a short walk down the street, or a bus ride will in such cases provide the information you seek.

It can be helpful to you to know the interests and principal areas of knowledge of all the people with whom you are acquainted, not only for the increased ability to remember their names, which will be discussed in a later section, but also in your occasional searches for information from reliable authorities. If the library is closed and you want to find out in what year Joe Louis won the world heavy-weight championship perhaps your friend Phil who is an avid boxing fan will be able to tell you. If you can't remember whether you're supposed to remove ink stains with milk or lemon jnice, a call to the local tailor, Mr. Jones, will provide the necessary advice. The people that you know, and with whom you do business, can often be of great assistance to you, when you're in need of some special information.

All that's required for you to utilize this invaluable source of information most efficiently is a knowledge of *who* can tell you *what* most reliably. An excellent example of where *paying attention* really pays off!

## Preparing "custom-tailored" memory-minimizers

Not every little bit of information which you decide you need can be located in books; and when you want to know something special, it's not always very convenient to obtain the assistance of someone who can tell you what you want to know. If you are able to anticipate which special information you're likely to desire, it's a good idea to *prepare* an appropriate memory-minimizer in advance, which can be conveniently stored, to be referred to when the need arises.

Some information, as in the case of a specially designed schedule or programme which you must follow, can come best from yourself. To operate by your schedule efficiently, it's desirable to have a reminder that will tell you what to do and in what order, until you've done it often enough so that you no longer have need of this *temporary* memory-minimizer.

## Everything in its place

The easiest method of consistently finding things which you've put away is to consistently put them away in their proper, assigned, never-changing place. Always keep your theatre tickets in the same pocket, and you'll never again have to fumble through curtain-time. Always put your pen in its holder on your desk, and you'll never be at a loss when you've got to write. Always keep your specially-prepared memory-minimizers in their assigned niches, and they'll never be impossible to find when you need them.

Many, many notebooks, charts, tables, schedules, lists and so forth can be sensibly and simply prepared, which will lessen the burden on your natural memory, and enable you to function properly and efficiently, without fear of forgetting important things. We'll go into a few of these in some detail now, and we'll also mention in passing some simple, but vital expedients—such as knowing where to find the memory-minimizer—for remembering how to use them.

## Collections

You might have trouble remembering the individual components
of a group of objects which comprise your hobby, or the inventory
of your store, or the garments which are included in your ward-
robe, or any group of things at all.

The simplest method of keeping a record of such information
is, of course, to write it down . . . but of course there's a lot more
to it than that! You'll have a lot less trouble locating particular
parts of your written memory-minimizer if you make sure to
follow a definite pattern, a carefully organized plan in your
notations.

If the curator of a museum were simply to enter in a little
notebook the title and artist's name of every canvas which was
added to his collection, as each was acquired, he'd have a rough
chore ahead of him each time he wanted to locate his entry for
any single painting—he'd have to read through his entire notebook, entry by entry, until he came upon the one for which he
was looking. If no such listing existed, he'd have to cover the
inventory from start to finish before he *found out* that it didn't
exist. And he wouldn't even be sure that he hadn't accidentally
skipped over it.

If, on the other hand, he kept his record on individual filing
cards, arranged alphabetically by artist, as well as by title and
subject, his search for a particular entry would be rapid and sure.
Imagine your own difficulty if the dictionary were merely an
unordered list of words!

For your own collection, of books . . . records . . . hats . . .
medals—most likely you need not go to the bother of preparing
individual cards to be filed in a special container, because your
"B's" and "K's" will be few enough so that you can enter them all
on a single page in a notebook. Remember, however, that as your
collection grows, diminishes through discarding and grows again,
your record of its components must be correspondingly altered.

So, depending on the collection's size and degree of "turnover", you've got to leave sufficient leeway in your notebook to take care of the changes.

When does this procedure of keeping a record of collections come in handy ? Well, the most obvious use for it is in connection with a collector's hobby—a record of the components of your collection will prove quite useful, when you collect things other than small items which are kept in a systematically organized album. As your collection grows, you find it increasingly difficult to keep track of the items of which it is composed, and when you come across a new recording of Bach's Second Brandenburg Concerto, you can't remember whether you already have one version of this piece in your record library. By checking your systematically-arranged record index, you discover that you do, and you can take it out and listen to it. In this way you'll be able to decide either to purchase the new one, because you prefer it, or save the money because your own recording is preferable.

If you have a library of reference books and others to which you occasionally turn for information, you'll save time when looking for something if you keep a record of its volumes; you can check your inventory to see if you're going to be able to locate the information you seek, before resorting to the time-consuming expedient of reading the titles of all your books, shelf by shelf.

You can even keep a handy record of the television shows you like best to watch, if you occasionally miss a favourite through oversight. This memory-minimizer will take a familiar form—just like the daily listings in the newspaper.

You might, if your family is large, or under-the-weather unusually often, keep a record of illnesses, prescriptions and medications, so that when Johnny catches a cold you can give him the pills which you bought last month to cure Susy's cold. Check with your doctor, to make sure that the pills are appropriate, and that they haven't lost their effectiveness by standing for too long a time in the medicine chest.

Whatever the special needs and considerations, there's an easy way of keeping a record of the items in your collection. If you're the purchasing agent for an office, you'll select the system which is most convenient and applicable for your particular organization; if you're a shopkeeper, you'll likewise resort to the most convenient method of keeping your records, if you're keeping an account of things for your own personal convenience, you'll select the simplest, surest method of doing so.

Can't you think of a few collections of your own that you'd like to categorize and keep "on record"? The procedure's simple, and the benefits which you'll derive will tell you at once whether it's worth your small effort.

You can decide for yourself just where to keep your specially prepared memory-minimizers—on the bookshelf, in a drawer of your desk, under the dining-room table—only be sure that you always keep it in the same place, so that you need not search for it when it's wanted.

## Names and numbers

You certainly don't keep eighteen telephone directories in your home just because you are acquainted with people in eighteen different cities. You've written down their names, addresses and telephone numbers in a notebook or some other volume which is especially designed for the listing of personal numbers.

And, like as not, you keep a pocket version of pretty much the same information on your person at all times. Are the entries which you've made arranged in a convenient order? Is there sufficient room to accommodate additional entries? Most name-and-number listing needs prescribe a first-initial-of-last-name alphabetical listing, with plenty of extra room for additions under each letter. The travelling salesman might profit by arranging his clients' numbers alphabetically within separate geographical sections, so that by referring to one entry he'll find himself at a page upon which other entries will remind him of other calls he must make.

The household personal telephone directory might be kept in a sort of modified "classified" fashion, if it's not inconvenient: Close friends, distant relatives, professional acquaintances, tradesmen, etc.

In the pages of your home directory you might want to keep a record of supplementary information, such as birthday and anniversary dates, distinguishing likes and dislikes, or anything else that might be of some use sometime. Provide a special, never-changing location for the book, and always return it to its place after using it.

## Important dates and appointments

You can write yourself little reminder notes about appointments, anniversaries, bill-paying dates and the like, leaving them haphazardly on one table or another, stuffing them in the pockets of one jacket or another, and hope that you'll bump into the note, by chance, just at the right time. Or you can organize your "paper secretary" into an ordered, systematic, practically foolproof programme for remembering special days and times.

The most important part of an appointment or special occasion is remembering when it's supposed to happen. And the most important feature of any programme for reminding yourself of special dates and times is its periodic *command* of your attention. The engagement calendar which sits on your desk at the office, the datebook you keep in your home, the memo pad in your pocket, will serve no purpose at all if they're not referred to regularly.

Get into the habit of looking at these reminders regularly, at specially designated times each day—the same special times every day. Should you make an appointment while you're away from your engagement pad, make a notation of it in your pocket memo, and try to transcribe the message to its proper spot on the calendar before too much time goes by. Make a habit of checking your notes just before the end of every day, so that you can keep your home records complete. Make a habit, too, of referring to your pocket memo at regular intervals during the day, so as not to miss any immediate reminders.

If it's convenient, a good method of reminding yourself about events and appointments is to post notes on a small bulletin board, mounted in a regularly conspicuous place. At home, you might keep the board in the bathroom, where you've got to go first thing every morning . . . or on the wall just to the side of the door by which you leave the house. Keep a pencil, and enough extra paper to take care of your needs, handy at all times.

Pick any spot at all to put up the bulletin board, as long as traffic past it is steadily heavy throughout the day. Should you decide, for instance, that the most appropriate spot would be the inside of the refrigerator, or the top of the television set, your bulletin board's unusual location might accentuate the impact of your reminder message.

Engagement calendar . . . pocket memo . . . bulletin board . . . take the one, or more than one, memory-minimizer which you feel most effectively and efficiently satisfies your need to be reminded of appointments . . . but be absolutely certain that it receives your attention regularly and often!

## Facts and figures

Since a greater understanding of any subject will inspire a stronger memory of it, a little bit must be said about efficient, organized study. A good studying technique will benefit anyone having a desire to learn and remember information about anything. The next few pages are of very special application to the student.

When some special project presents you with the task of compiling a great mass of information about a particular subject, you must often resort to the expedient of gleaning the most pertinent data from several sources. You may be required to refer to several books, magazine articles, and an authority or two, and you'll have to use your own powers of reasoning and organization in order to combine all that material into a meaningful unit.

When you've completed all your research, you'll come to the conclusion that it would be a lot less difficult to prepare a special report or notebook, than to carry around with you all those books, clippings and people. In fact, since you'd often find it impossible to retain under one roof all the sources you've used—library books, people, etc.—a concise report would be the only solution to your problem, short of committing all that material to natural memory!

Your notes, then, take on the characteristics and functions of a custom-built memory-minimizer—a specially-prepared device designed to circumvent natural memorization by providing a written account of factual information. But, while working to eliminate the need for memorizing, they service it practically without your noticing—the complication and organization of relevant material having provided you with an understanding of the total subject, such understanding being necessary for the construction of an intelligible summary!

In both compilation and review, summaries of factual information happily possess the bonus characteristic of providing a means of inspiration to your natural memory. For the student, a well-prepared collection of notes will provide invaluable guidance in his studies. For the businessman, charts, graphs and reports on conditions, growth, progress and so forth, will help to point out the trends and patterns which make him mentally more familiar with the information.

The use of an outline in the review and study of a subject is, in effect, a means of placing a "middle step" between impression and remembrance—*recognition*. The outline serves the purpose of providing your mind with a reproduction of the material for study—repetition which is so important in memorization.

And the more vivid, the more lucid, the more concise your "memory-stimulator", the more efficiently you'll be able to learn and retain the information you're studying. For the present, we'll consider only the actual preparation of outlines and summaries; their efficient use in study for memorizing will be discussed in a separate chapter of Section Four.

Outlines can be prepared to greatly varying degrees of completeness . . . reduce an 800-page textbook all the way down to its very simplest summation, and you are left with its three-word title! Even that small prompter will enable you to recognize something about the topic—will remind you of some little part of the reading that you've done.

A short step up from the prompting title you find the headings of the sections which present separate parts of the text's subject; then the chapter headings, bold-face subject heads, principal sentences of the most important paragraphs, selected paragraphs and even pages in their entirety . . . all the way back up to the total itself! For in order for the outline to fulfil its functions, it must be no less complete than is required to remind you of all the material for which you make it responsible.

Your own outline need not be as general as is the title, nor must it be as thorough as the total; but it must certainly be somewhere in-between, and that's the first thing you've got to decide upon when you're about to construct one—it's degree of thoroughness. Do you know enough, factually, about the subject so that a bare framework of major points will suffice to start your memory working, or will you need a little something more to recall more fully the factors which fill out the body of the topic? Can you get along allright with an organized list of key words and phrases, or would you be better off with short sentences? Will it be necessary for you to become familiar with the subject to an extremely thorough degree, or will just a cursory understanding sufficiently serve your purposes ?

Once you've decided upon the degree of completeness to which you're going to outline the subject, or the speech, or the activity, you are next faced with the problem of determining your source, or sources. Will you be able to gather all the necessary information from a single book, or might you have to refer to several? Will you find it necessary to seek the information and advice of people who know the subject better than you do? Will you find it necessary to perform an experiment or two in order to complete any phases of the information? Prepare a bibliography—not necessarily complete and unalterable, for you could discover a weak point in the midst of your preparations, but full enough to present in your research a good general picture.

And then research the subject. Take notes informally as you go along—you'll be able to judge how complete these must be as you do the work itself, by noting how fully you understand the material—and, keeping in mind the entire topic, jot down any random observations that come to you about each point you make in writing. The important thing, remember, is to understand what you're outlining as fully as possible, so that the outline can be kept concise, and yet retain its lucidity.

Your notes completed, you can then get down to the actual construction of a finished outline. A short time after the initial taking of notes, read through them short segments at a time, thinking of appropriate breakers—handles by which to classify and organize them. If it makes more sense to you to arrange your entries differently than they appear in your first draft, adjust them accordingly—for your prime purpose is, after all, to make sense. Refer back to the original sources whenever you fail to fully understand something in your notes. This expedient will serve to assure thoroughness in the review which you're undergoing as you prepare the outline.

Underscore the points which you deem of prime importance;

also those which you have found elusive. Assigning identifying numbers and letters to the sections and facts of your outline will often provide a little something extra which may come in handy when you must commit it to natural memory. In some special cases perhaps a rough sketch, graph or table will serve to make more vivid some part of the subject with which you're occupied.

And . . . when the entire summary is written down in black and white, make a point of reading it through from beginning to end, to make sure that you haven't left any part of it in a confused or ambiguous state.

Plan the entire outline in advance of its actual written preparation—consider its purposes, its derivations, its form, and degree of thoroughness—and follow it through carefully, never losing sight of the fact that *unless you see that it makes sense as you write it down, it won't make sense when you refer to it*. Construction of a summary will be valuable to you in just one important function—reminding you about things which you already understand.

So . . . memory-minimizers (and memory-stimulators) capitalize upon the basic memory principles of planning digestible tasks, writing-out and visualization, pattern and association, and repetition and review. It is also important that your mental faculties be "tuned in" to what's being covered. Pretty much the same qualities which are required for the strengthening of your natural memory, aren't they?

Both natural and artificial memory—often in combination—have their respective places in combating problems in individual areas of memorization. Your need to "remember" names, for instance, will in some cases be handled satisfactorily with an artificial device, while at other times it will be necessary for you to spend the time required for natural memorization. For some people a brief outline of the facts which bear upon a specific topic will suffice, while for others a thorough working knowledge of the subject is necessary, for business, self-satisfaction, or whatever may inspire the need.

The closing section of this book will deal in both ways with several specific areas of memory utilization. It will suggest suitable, efficient methods of applying memory principles to individual problems, for both natural and artificial remembering, leaving to you the choice of which alternative is preferable.

# SECTION FOUR

*How to strengthen your memory of—*

*Informal discussions of the treatment of specific memory problems, pointing out efficient and effective ways of utilizing the principles governing ability to remember—naturally, and artificially.*

# 7

## THE INFORMATION WHICH COMES
## FROM READING

VERY few things are more exasperating than getting into a discussion about a novel which you've only recently finished reading, and then to discover that you're somehow unable to recall the name of the place in which all the action took place, the nickname of the killer's second victim, the year of the plague, or any one of lots of other facts that ought to be right on the tip of your tongue. And the very same annoyance can prevail when the same thing happens with all kinds of books—from detective stories to detailed treatises on physics.

Having completed a book in which you were really quite interested while you did the reading, and yet being at a loss when it comes to discussing it intelligently, you will naturally blame your "lousy memory" . . . but, after all, while you were reading you were anxious to get to the part where the principal action is resolved—you hurried through what could have been pages and pages of interesting reading, because you could hardly wait to find out "who did it," or what was going to happen to the principal characters, or whether you'd be able to apply that cantilever principle in the plans for the scale model railway you were building.

## Reading for fun

Most pleasure books—or, at least most of those which are worth discussing—are so much more than mere tales, adventures and anecdotes. The author of a worthwhile book has researched his subject or plot thoroughly . . . made sure to avoid errors, anachronisms or impossible situations . . . taken care to develop the characters meaningfully and realistically . . . carefully selected and depicted appropriate settings and locales for his story. Each word in his manuscript has some connection, either inherent in the story itself or somewhere in the back of his mind, with the direction and aim of the total work.

Once conscious of this, you'll hardly find it possible to skip over large segments of any book again, because you'll realize that by so doing you'd be missing so great a part of its total pattern and meaning.

The first objective in pleasure-reading is, of course, the derivation of pleasure; don't bother to plough through pages and pages of prose that holds no interest for you—don't waste your time looking at meaningless words, for if you're not interested in what you're reading, you can't expect them to convey any message.

But, if you feel that a particular book is worthwhile, you'll want to find some means of attaching inspiration for your interest to the long segments of narrative which aren't absolutely vital to the resolution of the part of the plot in which you're interested.

## Playing the role

Soon after you've begun reading a novel, select a character whose life you think might be interesting to lead—in your imagination —and every once in a while as you progress through the pages, pause for a few moments to reflect and "re-live" the events which have just been described to you. Imagine what your reactions would be to the situations and experiences of the character, and try to "get into" his or her mind.

Thus you'll be reviewing, using your memory actively in imagination, visualizing, forming a pattern and digesting the novel small bits at a time, all in this one simple activity. And each episode, each otherwise not-too-terribly-interesting portion of the narrative will take on a new dimension, a personal attribute which will serve to sustain your interest through every word.

## Keeping a record

On the inside of the cover of the book, or on one or more of the blank pages at its front or back, write down the name of each character you meet within the chapters, his identifying characteristics, and his relationships to other characters and the story as a whole. Write down a synopsis of the scenes and locales as the story progresses. Keep a brief, concise record of the romantic, antagonistic and other assorted entanglements between the characters. Make random observations about the behaviour of the characters, and about the development of the action.

These informal tables of information, easy to prepare and forever made a part of the volume, will help you to refresh your memory each time you pick up the book to continue your reading, reminding you where you left off when last you put it down. They will combine to become an outline of the total piece, ideal for casual review, helpful in reinforcing your understanding of the story, unequalled as something to help you decide, some time in the future, whether you'd like to read the book again.

## Comparisons to other reading

Every book you read will afford comparisons between itself and other reading you've done—comparisons of style, of character development, of locale, of plot treatment, and so forth. By looking for such associations you're not only refreshing the memory of the impressions which you received from the words in the book you just finished reading, but you're also constructing comparative handles by which you can remember worthwhile ideas and parts of it, and multiplying your familiarity with its total, as well as your potential contribution to any discussion about it and related works. Further, you're developing more fully your personal taste, and your ability to make critical judgements.

And the more you're able to "do" with a subject—the more deeply you become personally, intellectually involved—the more completely you'll be able to enjoy yourself with it, and, consequently, the more closely you'll find yourself paying attention.

It shouldn't be too difficult, now, to devise a practicable method of inspiring your greater interest in reading which doesn't fall into the classification of narrative. In the previous chapter a little bit was said about the proper preparation of outlines; when it becomes necessary—for business, or for school, or for some social obligation—to learn a subject thoroughly, such outlines become guides which are practically indispensable for study and memorization. But for pure pleasure, without an absolute need for thorough learning, a much simpler alternative will generally do.

There are usually a few blank pages, at the front or rear of every book, or on the inside of the covers. If not, there's no law against using a little paste and notepaper. If a book isn't your own, use a few sheets of paper as a bookmark. The use of these pages in connection with "condensing" the material of a novel has already been pointed out; no less useful are they in providing convenient reminders for your mind when you read other books.

Record brief statements of important and interesting facts, and reinforce them with page numbers, so that you can turn back to the text if you like. Write down briefly your own observations about relative points, connections between current material and other personal knowledge—anything that occurs to you as you read. Within the text itself, don't hesitate to underline passages or sentences or words which strike you vividly, and feel free to make notes and comments in the margins. When you come upon two or more points which strengthen each other in their relationship, draw arrows between them, or, if they're on different pages, jot down their page numbers alongside their related facts. To record the same kind of information while you're reading a library book, improvise on notepaper.

Your in-the-book outline need not be anything overwhelmingly elaborate—for that matter, the outline which you prepare in a special notebook to assist you in thorough learning of material can be rather simple, too. Both serve only to prod your natural memory, and both need be only as complicated as is necessary to call to your mind, *to the extent you want them to*, as much material as you desire.

## Facilitating study with an outline

In the consideration of thoroughly learning and memorizing material, it must first be understood that your outline is intended to serve two purposes: first, to condense the task by eliminating all the information which you deem unnecessary, and reducing the facts to clear, understandable terms; second, to induce your mind itself to elaborate on those simplest terms, thus constructively adding depth and dimension to the basic framework.

But you knew all that when you prepared the outline, and now it's time to efficiently put it to practical use. Begin by assuming, as nearly as possible, ideal conditions under which to work—Are you wide awake and alert? Have you satisfactorily convinced yourself that nothing is at the moment so important that it might prevent you from giving it your full attention? Are you comfortable where you sit, and in the clothes you're wearing? Is the lighting sufficient? Have you taken care to reduce noises and potential interruptions to a minimum? Have you placed at hand everything you could possibly need during your study, so that you won't find any excuses for leaving it once you've begun?

Are you ready now? You had prepared your outline by working your way out, from the very heart of the material to the barest framework. Now, you'll work your way in, from the superstructure to the core. Read the outline through once, as quickly as you can without losing any of its general meaning. Don't, for the moment, concentrate on particulars, statistics, precise explanations of facts and concepts; but, rather try to present to yourself a general overall picture of the total—a backdrop, as it were, upon which you can see a pattern and a direction.

Now, introduce that bonus element of extra rewards. Do you like to take a cup of tea or coffee occasionally in your studies? Is there a chocolate layer cake in the kitchen? Plan to work at the outline in informally regulated periods, taking time out once in a while to have a drink or a snack, or anything you decide upon as your bonus.

Start in by reading only the things you've designated as the broadest subject-markers, reflecting leisurely as you go along, repeating each item as much as you like, trying to "fill in" the skeleton with material dredged up out of your natural memory's storehouse.

When you've completed your review and reflection at this broad level, take a few minutes off to reward yourself for good behaviour . . . but just a few. Then return to work; proceed to the next level of thoroughness that is featured in your outline—sub-heads, breakers or what-have-you. Follow the very same procedure that you did with the broader headings—permitting your own mind to fill in whatever facts it's able to remember. And work your way gradually, all the way in to the heart of the outline, level by level. Pause whenever you find it necessary, and retrace your steps to clarify individual points.

If you must, refer back to your original sources, but never do this before you've tried as hard as you can to call the material naturally to mind. In this manner you'll be giving your mind the active exercise it wants, and reviewing the material in the most constructive possible way—you'll be allowing your mind to teach itself!

And when all that reviewing, repeating, reinforcing and rewarding has filled your mind with facts and your stomach with goodies, read the entire outline once again—from start to finish—just to prove that you know what you've been thinking about. Make sure you know all of the material quite well . . . and then put in ten minutes more! Overlearning pays off in dividends far greater than your investment—a little bit of overlearning will go a long, long way.

Remember to avoid, as much as possible, the memory-disturbing interference which grows out of your following study with some similar type of mental activity. You're less likely to forget things while you're sleeping than during conscious, active hours . . . so, if you find that you're able to do your studying in the evening, just before retiring—without having to worry about fatigue—you might be better off. Consider each element that can affect your studying—the degree of your alertness, potential interference from subsequent activity, possibilities of being interrupted, external noise . . . anything and everything which can add to or detract from your efficient use of study time. When you've hit upon your most efficient times, places and schemes of study, endeavour to make them a habit.

Virtually all reading is "for fun", if you approach it in the right frame of mind. All that's required is a little bit of thinking, to find some connection between the material in the reading and those things with which you're already familiar, the things in which you're naturally interested. If you fetch far enough, any subject can be brought into relationship with practically any other—and in a manner which will genuinely arouse your interest and curiosity.

And with the assistance of one or two of the expedients which are outlined in this chapter, as well as a few you're sure to think of on your own, you'll be well able to assure yourself a worthwhile consumption of knowledge from every page you read!

# 8

## SPEECHES, ANECDOTES AND
## OTHER RECITATION

IT might happen that you're called upon to deliver an important address to an enormous audience from a raised podium . . . or you might simply be involved in telling a joke or anecdote to a group of friends . . . making a committee report to the membership of your social club . . . lecturing your child on the habits of "the birds and the bees" . . . or reciting in class on the day's lesson. Each of these examples represents, for our present purposes, a "speech" of sorts, and each can be made simpler, less tedious and more fun, through just a little bit of efficient preparation.

First, decide whether the information which you are going to be transmitting must be delivered verbatim, or merely told in an informal manner, in the words of the moment. Most often you'll find that it isn't absolutely necessary to commit a speech or story to verbatim memory . . . and your speech will be more interesting, easier to follow, when you speak with an understanding of the subject. Understanding is necessary when you make a speech from a bare outline of points, for you'll find that in order to convey your intended meaning without merely reciting by rote you'll have to follow the recitation yourself.

## Speeches in the words of the moment

It's safe to assume that every recitation with which you are likely to become involved will consist of a series of points and facts surrounding a general overall theme. The first thing to do in preparing your recitation, therefore, is to isolate, clarify and plainly identify the theme. Then each individual point in the outline of the speech will have some concrete bearing upon the pattern of the whole, and you'll be able to visualize it within the speech's entire framework.

Prepare an outline of the material in very much the same way as has already been discussed in connection with study outlines. To do this, you'll probably find it helpful to write out a rough draft of the entire speech, word for word, although you don't intend to deliver it verbatim. Underline important words, phrases and passages, insert appropriate headings and sub-heads where they serve to set off important thoughts and ideas, and read through the entire speech several times. It's at least as important to study the total, giving yourself a good understanding of the full picture, as it is to work on individual parts of the subject outline for vivid memorization.

Work down from your verbatim speech to a clear, concise, vivid outline. Concentrate in your study upon the logical development of ideas, noting how one sentence leads logically to the next, how one idea lays a foundation and basis for ensuing statements. Finally, work extra-hard on the individual parts which give you the most trouble, without however losing sight of the specific place they occupy in the total speech. Where necessary, divise association chains of key words, phrases and thoughts, to help you in the transition from one point to the next.

Know your subject and theme—understand yourself what you're trying to impart to your listeners; know the direction in which you intend to travel—have a very good idea of the development and organization of your speech, so as to avoid that confused rambling which tends to put an audience to sleep. With these two main problems under your control, you can't help presenting your material efficiently, clearly and understandably.

You're probably not going to make friends or influence people by starting to tell a funny story and having your memory run down just short of the punch line! But, if you're like nearly everyone else, you certainly *enjoy* telling anecdotes, jokes and stories among friends.

When you hear a joke that you'd like to be able to repeat later, *pay special attention to the punch line.* Create an association between it and the place you've heard it, because you're likely to remember that, at least. Visualize the action which takes place . . . unusual, improbable or outrageous. You can always reconstruct a funny story by working back from the laughter.

### Verbatim recitation—poetry, quotations, etc.

Word-for-word memorization of recitation becomes necessary when you are called upon to recite certain things verbatim, or when you feel that the phrasing of a specific point or passage in a speech is particularly vivid, strong or effective. The punch-line of an anecdote will sometimes lose its effect unless stated in a specific word-for-word manner.

Commission to memory of exact passages requires a great deal more study and repetition than does learning an outline, and introduces the risk of your speaking by rote, without really understanding, yourself, what you're saying. The most important consideration, then, is to assure yourself that you understand the passage you're memorizing. Do this by analyzing the words and phrases themselves, and trying to put their ideas and meanings into other words while you're studying them. In order to "say the same thing" in different words, you must first completely understand the meaning of the passage.

The length of the passage to be memorized will be a deciding factor in the question of memorizing in sections or as a whole. If the piece is very long, you'll find it impossible to memorize it as a single thing with much efficiency. However, dividing it into sections introduces the risk of losing sight of the overall pattern. Decide with each individual problem which method to use. When you must first break a long passage down into easier-to-handle sections, follow the system of associating the sections, one with the other, that has already been outlined.

Every device for memorization which has been heretofore discussed in this book—paired associates, association chains, visualization, etc.—is fair play in preparing speeches and other recitation for tongue-tip. Prime importance must be designated, however, to your understanding of the material . . . when you know what you're talking about, associations work better, ideas fall more clearly into patterns, and, just in case your memory fails you, you'll be able to fall back on the good old knowledge which is stored in your mind.

# 9

## NUMERICAL THINGS

IT'S sad to say, but when it comes to memorization, there's really very little safety in numbers . . . for numbers are abstract things, and they make themselves very difficult to be remembered until they can be associated with other, more concrete concepts. When a date, a price, a business figure is connected through mental association with something familiar, it then becomes workable in your scheme of memory. But, left alone as a mere isolated digit or group of linear wriggles, there isn't very much that can be done with it for memory's sake.

The first thing you're likely to see in a number is some sort of pattern—a design in its construction which might enable you to recall or recognize it the next time it crosses your path. "1234" forms a simple pattern . . . so do "1357", "5555", "368", and so forth.

And you can, if you like, or if you must, see patterns in numbers that aren't so obvious—it's not important that the pattern be one which enables you to categorize the number among well-known classifications such as odd-even-odd-even, or descending-steps-of-two. The fact that "27" plus "6" produces "33" provides a pattern in "2733" . . . "3412" induces you to think that "3" times "4" equals "12". Any analysis that you can make of a number's construction, such as the numerical difference between its digits, or its ascent and descent, will provide one more associative feature, still on the abstract level, but an associative hook never-theless.

The next feature that might occur to you in analyzing a number is the existence of some special association between it and another part of your own knowledge—"1492" brings something specific to mind, and, should this number be someone's address, you're not likely to have much trouble remembering it.

The associations which you see in numbers will depend upon your particular personal fund of knowledge. To one person "1849" might signify the square of "43", while to another, it might bring to mind the famous California Gold Rush. Did you know that "289" is the square of "17" . . . that "34" is the number of shots fired at the legendary gunfight at the O.K. Corral . . . that "39.37" is the number of inches in a metre ?

Your own particular basic fund of knowledge will also come in handy in another manner, when you're working with numbers. You're not likely to believe that that new car you're thinking of buying will cost you no more than £70, because your basic knowledge of current prices and values will enable you to place the other nought in its proper place.

Perhaps the most useful single device for enabling you to remember numerical things is that of number-letter (or word) translation. You remember our previous examples of translating numbers into associatable words, first, through the alphabetical order—A-1, B-2, C-3, etc., and then by using the specially devised table of number-letter values and key association words. In the case of telephone numbers, at least, a third translation system is sometimes readily available—the numbers may be replaced by any one of the three letters which share their particular designations on the dial. Thus, the number "7" can be translated to "P", "R" or "S" . . . the number "2" might become "A", "B" or "C". And, if the digits "0" and "1" are absent from any particular telephone number, a word which is less difficult to remember than that string of digits can be devised and "dialled" in its stead. For instance, if you want to speak to someone whose phone number is "HOV 3047", rather than dialling the number, you can dial "H-O-T-D-O-G-S".

You've got some leeway in the construction of these words, with as many as three letters to choose from for each digit. You can even, if you like, trade in the exchange letters for more readable ones. You don't even have to form real words, for mere pronounceable syllables will provide a more easily-remembered pattern than do the numbers themselves.

So . . . you've got three distinctively different, yet really quite similar methods of translating numbers into the more familiar forms which letters and words will afford . . . to say nothing of any number of systems which you yourself can devise. Try all of the systems with every numerical problem that comes along, if you like, and determine which one provides the most beneficial association for each particular case.

With all of these patterns, associations with your personal knowledge and devices for translation, there's still only one way to be absolutely certain of remembering factual figures, and that's knowing and understanding the facts behind the figures. If you're well-versed in information about the trends which have influenced your business during the past few weeks, you'll have at your command a very good framework within which to fit the numbers you're trying to remember. If you know that a particular building is located on Avenue "A" between "B" Street and "C" Street, and that the system of address-numbering in that neighbourhood involves ascending numbers from "100", you'll be fairly certain that the address of the building in question is probably something between "100" and "150". If you are aware of the fact that young Will Shakespeare lived during the late Sixteenth and early Seventeenth Centuries, and that he participated as an actor in a play by Ben Jonson, you will be sure that Jonson was born in 1573, and not 1753.

Here are examples of several methods which you might use to

anchor in your memory a given number. Suppose that in your company's catalogue, item number "432" is a beautiful ukulele. First of all, if you know that the 400's in the stock-number system are set aside for musical instruments, you're already one-third of the way home. And if you've studied the catalogue sufficiently you have probably come to know the number and its stock item through simple repetition. At any rate, it can't hurt you to provide for your memory's sake the additional hooks which are available through the several translation systems.

When translating the number, "432", with the code-key which was outlined 'way back in Chapter Five, you arrive at "R-M-N" . . . these letters may be fashioned into the word "harmony", which can easily be associated with the stock item. Alphabetically, the numbers translate into "D-C-B" . . . with these letters you might contrive a simple sentence, such as "Dogs Crave Bones," and then associate a bone-craving dog with the famous flea-bearer of ukulele fame—"My dog has fleas." From the telephone dial you might come up with "I-D-A" from the catalogue number, and visualize a pretty girl named Ida, wearing a grass skirt and strumming a ukulele.

You're not likely to confuse the product of one translation system with that of another, because when you try the systems mentally you probably won't grab at what you come up with unless it strikes a familiar chord.

As far as inherent pattern, the number "432" contains an immediately recognizable one . . . and, if "432" happens to be the last half of your automobile license plate, you've got an additional association from your personal fund of knowledge.

Having a rough idea of the area in which the number you're looking for falls, and having provided through association and translation a few extra hooks by which to recall it, you'll be in a fairly good position to remember it. As long as you're using your mind for thinking, as well as for devising and playing tricks, your memory for numerical things will stand you in good stead.

# 10

## PEOPLE ... THEIR NAMES AND FACES

A PICKLE, by any other name, would taste as dill . . . but it's a lot easier to convey the idea to someone by saying "pickle", than by telling him about a long, lumpy green thing that's got little tiny seeds inside and tastes sour and salty. Names are, after all, nothing more than convenient identifying titles which we give to people, so that we won't get confused between the president of the bank and the nuisance on the next street.

The problem of remembering people's names is a threefold task: remembering the people . . . remembering the names . . . and connecting the right names with the right people. And what's the best way to go about solving the problem? It's the same old story all over . . . you'll find yourself better able to remember things when you take a greater interest in thcm! Names will make deeper impressions upon your memory when you know more about their derivations and development. Faces will be more familiar to your sight when you look for unusual features and distinguishing characteristics. Names and faces will hang together in your memory when the people behind them are better known to you.

When you know a person only slightly, his name will tend to make vivid your concept of his personality and physical appearance, because you've associated it with him. But once you've got to know him better, the name becomes less vital to your remembrance of him, because you're able to mentally picture him and many of your experiences with him. At the same time, your memory of his name becomes more and more important, since you're more and more likely to have the opportunity of using it—in addressing him, introducing him to other people, and in speaking about him.

The point is that it's important to build your memory of a person's name as early as possible in your relationship, when your reliance upon the name itself is greatest. Resort to the memory principles which have already proved themselves invaluable to your efficient memorization of all things—pattern, and association.

There are patterns in names—in their spelling (Adam, Willis, Anne)... in their rhythm (CYN-thi-a PAT-ter-son, seg-is-MUN-do quin-ON-es)... in their appropriateness to their owners (twins named Harry and Barry, a fat man named Gross and a thin man named Little). Many names provide convenient bases for visualization and association—first names such as Robin, Samson, Lily and Rock furnish obvious images and/or associations; surnames such as Bonaparte, Field, Silver and Farmer do the same.

In many names the imagery and association might not be so evident, but they are always present just the same. Bernard is derived from a bear; Rex means king; Jacqueline is "following after"; Gertrude means spear-maiden; Edith means rich gift·

Still another group of names that have been selected by parents in honour of popular celebrities, provide association through the memories of the celebrities themselves: names which have recently increased in use because of popular movie and television idols include Milton, Gary, Brigitte, Glenn, Loretta, Deborah and Cary. The same kind of association with a famous namesake is available in biblical names, as well as in names of family ancestors.

## The derivation of surnames

Unless you've got some kind of working knowledge of derivations of surnames, such apparently unvisual ones as Mendelssohn, Stark, Canero and Delgado will convey very little to you that can be used associatively. A little bit of background is therefore desirable—just a few morsels to whet your interest's appetite, and thus bring you to pay attention more fully whenever you come across new names.

If in nominal respect at least you're just like everyone else—and you are—your last name is originally derived in one or more of four ways: by the trade or occupation of some ancestor, such as John the Smith or Richard the Miller; by an ancestor's residence, as in James (near the) Hill or Thomas (by the) Stonewall; by a forerunner's nickname, like Samuel (the) Strong or Harry (the) Hardy; by the name of a parent or patron, such as Charles Richardson (Richard's son) or Patrick Fitzgerald (son of Gerald).

Surnames which originated in foreign countries and which, appropriately enough, are made of words of a foreign tongue, might sound as if they were just made up out of a bunch of letters, but they were built in exactly the same way as Cook and Butler and Field and Strong and Johnson.

TRADE'S NAMES

German: Zimmerman (carpenter)
French: Fermier (farmer)
Spanish: Canero (plumber)
Italian: Cavallo (horseman)

RESIDENTIAL NAMES

Spanish: Rivera (by the river)
German: Frankfurter (from Frankfurt)
French: Rousseau (at the brook)

NICKNAMES

German: Stark (strong)
Spanish: Delgado (thin)
French: Hardi (bold)
Italian: Tintoretto (dyer)

PATRONYMICS (FATHER'S NAMES)

German: Mendels*sohn*
French: *de* Jean or Pierre-*fils*
Spanish: Mend*ez*
Hebrew: *Ben* Yehudi
Irish: *Fitz*simmons, *O'*Hara, *Mc*Michaels
Greek: Parmen*ides*
Chinese: Lao-*tse*
Arabic: *ibn* Saud
Polish: Trot*ski*
Russian: Ivano*vitch*, Rachmanin*off*
Danish: Cornelli*sen*

Once you know a little bit about how names have come to take their forms, you're bound to note with an introduction to each new one the characteristics which make it unique. The whole subject is really very interesting, and it will provide bonus hooks for every new name you come across.

When someone is introduced to you, make sure right at the start that you have got his name correctly. Unless you know how to spell it you won't be able to visualize it written out, so don't hesitate to ask how it's spelled. Repeat the name out loud as often as possible during your initial conversation. Say "How do you do, Mr. Jones," and "It was so nice meeting you, Mr. Jones." And if Mr. Jones is an acquaintance you'd like to keep, write down his name in your address book when you get the chance.

Your address book—that record you keep of people that you

meet—will be an invaluable aid in enabling you to remember names. You recall that in efficiently and beneficially preparing it you made a point of providing space in which to enter, next to each name, little bits of information about personality, likes and dislikes, and so forth. Well, if you were really interested in Mr. Jones, you discovered several of his traits by observing him and asking questions during your first encounter with him. Now's the time to make a note of his habit of chewing on the stem of his pipe, his horn-rimmed glasses, the high pitch of his voice, and the fact that he's married and has three children. And if you browse through your address book occasionally, your impression of Mr. Jones, anchored to his name, will become more solidly imbedded in your mind.

Analyze each name you meet—note whether it's long or short, whether or not it contains double-letters and diphthongs (double vowel sounds), whether it begins with a vowel or consonant, whether the name is derived from a trade or residence, it's probable national origin, whether or not the first name seems to "match" the surname . . . everything that you can observe about every single name will intensify its impression upon your memory.

Occasionally, even with names that are familiar and people whom you know and like quite well, you might draw a mental block when it comes to making an introduction or otherwise having to use them. Stall as best you can—cough, comment upon the weather, or faint—and mentally run through the alphabet, letter by letter. Try to think back to some time in the past when you and the elusive-named one were together and you had occasion to call him by his or her name. In reacting that past event mentally, you might just dupe your brain into releasing the missing information. Failing to refresh your memory with either of these devices, just remember that I, for one, am glad that it's you and not me!

In brief, this is how you might go about strengthening your

memory for people and their names and faces: You're on the beach, say, relaxing in the sun, when an old friend named Frank Polvino sees you from across a crowded dune. He's been sitting there with another of his friends, and the two of them come over to you to say hello. As you see them coming, you realize that your name-saying mind is absolutely blank.

You recognize Frank immediately, of course, because you've known him for quite some time. But you had been lying in the sun day-dreaming, and your mind isn't very responsive for a moment. Now, it's not that you're going to flip through a mental file of name-and-face stock characteristics and immediately come up with the desired name . . . but, if you've learned the name and analyzed it, your mind will tend to remember it more readily, in proportion to the amount of analysis the name has undergone.

Polvino—it's an Italian name. This fellow coming towards you . . . one time you had dinner—ravioli—at his home. His name has been derived from the occupation of an ancestor—a wine-maker, and a rough translation of the name is "wine-pole". When you first learned the name you noted that it ended in a vowel, one which appeared earlier in its spelling. His entire name? FRANK-lin pol-VIN-o. But everyone calls him Frank. The rhythm inherent in the name brought to mind the first part.

Of course you realize that you didn't just sit there in the sand thinking about all these things as he walked towards you . . . undoubtedly all of this analysis occurred, if at all, at a subconscious level, and in less time than it took you to perceive his image. But because you had at one time taken the trouble to think about these things, the name itself became more vivid to you, and thus stuck firmly in your memory.

Now . . . what about this new person, the friend to whom Frank is about to introduce you? As you get up to greet them, you listen to Frank saying "Such-and-such, I'd like you to meet my very good friend, Cedric Beauregard". Immediately your empirical mind goes into action . . . CED-ric BEAU-re-gard. Rhythm tells you that the first syllable of each name is accented. The first name reminds you of a British actor, the last, of a Kentucky colonel on his plantation. Perhaps from the South of England? The first name begins and ends with the same letter. Beauregard is of French derivation, roughly meaning good-looking, if you want to translate literally. And if Cedric is especially good-looking, or especially bad-looking, you'll be able to vividly associate the name with the face. Three vowels in a row in the last name produce the pronounced sound of still a fourth. See anything else in the name?

The first thing that you say when you're introduced to this new person is "Hi, Cedric," or "How do you do, Mr. Beauregard" . . . depending on the tenor of the moment. During the next few minutes, in your conversation with this new acquaintance, you'll make a point of mentioning the name at least once more. If you find it impossible to do this because you didn't get the name clearly, either wait for Frank to use it, or ask! Cedric can be nothing but flattered that you thought his name important enough to want to get it correctly.

While you're speaking, you'll be busy noticing any distinguishing characteristics which Cedric might possess . . . deep-set eyes, receding hairline, square jaw, hairy arms, foreign accent, unusual height (large or small), and so forth. If a convenient association between his name and his physical appearance occurs to you, so much the better.

Finally, when you get back home and finish putting sunburn salve on your back, you'll make a note in your address book about your new acquaintance . . . his name itself, and anything else that you feel will be worth writing down. If the information eludes you, you can consult Frank, a convenient authority. And the next time you browse through the address book you'll be reinforcing your memory of Cedric Beauregard.

With just a bit of simple practice, you'll soon adopt the habit of automatically seeing patterns, associations and distinguishing characteristics in names. Even if you don't take a great interest in people themselves, your newly-developed interest in their names and faces will very shortly have you remembering these things to beat the proverbial band!

# 11

## HOW WORDS ARE SPELLED

For all you know, you might have one of the worst memories for spelling in the world, without having ever received the slightest hint that it's so! If you've spelled words incorrectly in your writing it has been because you don't know how to spell them in the correct way . . . so how are you going to realize that your mistakes are mistakes? Very seldom will someone to whom you've written a note or letter correct your errors in spelling and return your manuscript.

As for the existence of steadfast rules and regulations for proper spelling, or phonetic assistance from pronunciation in the English language, don't even begin to give either of those things a thought! How can you expect to receive any help from a language that deems correct such ambiguous contradictions as "to", "too" and "two" . . . "receive" and "believe" . . . "there", "their" and "they're" . . . "cough", "enough", "through", "dough" and "drought". How can you take seriously the reliability of rules for spelling in a language that says it's all right to say "kissable", but not "permissable" . . . "averring", but not "reverring"?

The best way to discover whether or not your memory for spelling is in need of improvement is to proof-read all of the writing that you do . . . with a dictionary! And, just to make sure that you're not passing over mistakes that you don't think of as mistakes, let someone else have a look at your written words once in a while. If you discover that you've been doing a lot of misspelling, take advantage of your memory, and use it to straighten things out.

The most effective way to strengthen your memory of how words are spelled is to read an awful lot. The more often you treat your eyes to the sight of words which are constructed of the proper letters in the proper order, the better you'll become at spelling words correctly yourself. At the same time you'll be introducing yourself to new words, thus strengthening your vocabulary, and words in the contexts of a variety of phrases and sentences, thus strengthening your knowledge of how they're properly used.

When you come across a word that you've spelled incorrectly, resort to "negative practice" for righting your error. Quite often your misspellings are already a habit, and the most effective way to break a habit is to bring it into conscious focus; then, when you do it, it's intentional, rather than habitual.

How does this work in correcting spelling errors? Let's assume that you've misspelled the word "judge" by leaving out the "d". Take a pencil in your hand, and write out

juge . . . that's stupid . . . juggy . . . joog . . .
juge . . . that's silly
juge . . . that's wrong
juge . . . juge . . . juge . . .

Write the word out in just the way that you had incorrectly written it before, several times, and with each "return to the crime" give yourself a mental slap on the wrist. Then, write

juDge . . . "D" in the middle . . .
juDge . . . nuDge . . . leDge . . . heDge . . .
juDge . . . juDge . . . juDge . . .

The visual trick of using a capital "D" can be modified to vividly point out the spelling errors which you make with many other words:

If you've misspelled "expense" by replacing the "s" with a "c", you might indicate this with "expenSe".

If you've written "dining" with an extra "n", you might use these gimmicks—"din(n)ing" . . . diNing".

If you've written "Wensday" instead of "Wednesday", you might try "weD-NES-day".

If the "ei" in "receive" gives you trouble—"rec(I)EIve".

Concentrate on the specific letter or letters which give you trouble, and repeat your practice of correcting your errors as much as you can. Perhaps you'll be able to set aside a special period of each day for working on spelling, until you feel that you've accomplished a reasonable degree of accuracy.

Instead of turning to the overabundant lists of "commonly misspelled words" which are found in textbooks and commercial spelling rectifier books, prepare *your own* list of the words which *you* misspell, by entering each one you come upon in your writing in a special notebook. Why spend time ridding yourself of other people's errors? You'll have enough to do with just your own!

# 12

## VOCABULARY AND FOREIGN LANGUAGES

IF you were to glance over the following list of words—

jable
usufruct
cascote
forse
flagellum
asticote

—would you be able to say for sure just which languages they come from? Two of those words are English! Can you pick them out?

Because, after all, every word which you don't understand is foreign to you, the methods you'd use to improve your command of words in the English language are precisely the same methods that you'd use in learning a foreign tongue. And so both of these problems will be considered simultaneously in this chapter.

Words are, once again, only symbols—of things . . . of activities . . . of values and ideas. You need them only to facilitate communication, with others, and sometimes with yourself. In order to understand the meaning of a word, you must be able to link it *directly* with its meaning—not indirectly, through another word. When you hear or read the word "blue" you should be able to think of the colour itself, and not "the colour of the clear sky in daylight," as the dictionary tells us. When you read or hear the French *"bleu"*, you must be able to think of the colour, without first translating the word to its English counterpart.

Hence the words that you want to learn, if they are to be genuinely comprehensible to you solely in themselves, ought to be studied in the context of meaningful material. It won't be good enough for you to study lists of words and their synonyms or brief definitions—you've got to see how they're used in speech and in prose . . . you've got to be able to visualize and understand their connotations.

It wouldn't pay for you to study the entire dictionary, for it contains many words that will never be of any use to you. Besides, you are already familiar with a good many of its entries.

When you come upon a vocabulary list for a foreign language, several of the words it contains will be easy for you to learn almost immediately—the German *"reflektor"*, *"hier"* (here), *"apfel"* and many others are either identical to the English in pronunciation, or quite similar. The same point can be made, regarding both spelling and pronunciation, about the words of other languages.

So . . . to make things more convenient and efficient, probably the best method of studying vocabulary words is with a stack of individual cards. You can include in your personal word-file as many cards as you like, removing the ones you've learned sufficiently and introducing new ones as you progress.

On one side of the card, in large letters, write down the word that you want to learn. On the other side, in very, very little letters down in a corner, write its definition or translation. Fill the rest of that side with a rough sketch that conveys the meaning of the word visually—for "dog", a picture of a dog . . . for "run", a picture of someone running . . . for "red", perhaps just a mark with a red crayon.

When using the cards for study, look first at the "question" side, and try to provide the "answer" from memory. Turn the card over and look at the picture. Use the word in a sentence, both orally and in writing. The next time you come to that card, use the word in a different sentence.

After a while, you'll be able to do entirely without the word-for-word answer, and think directly of the visual rendition of the word you're studying. Repetition of your card-flipping, and variety in your contextual sentences will soon fill the gap in your vocabulary.

Utilize spaced learning for studying vocabulary—you might carry a handful of cards around with you, to refer to whenever you've got a few spare moments—waiting for a bus, during lunch, etc. Give yourself time between study sessions, to find new uses for the words you're studying, in everyday language or in reading.

# 13

## THINGS YOU'VE GOT TO DO

THIS special classification of memory problems includes appointments you've got to keep, promises you've made, chores you've got to do, hiding-places in which you've put things, hazards you've got to avoid, and getting rid of anxiety over wondering whether you've taken care of things.

Your memory for a good many of these things can be considerably strengthened by the utilization of artificial reminders—you can make entries in a regularly-referred-to appointment calendar ... you can leave a note for yourself in a conspicuous place ... you can leave the clothes you've got to take to the tailor out somewhere in plain sight ... you can set the alarm clock or leave instructions with your secretary.

Take good advantage of all these opportunities to assure yourself of doing the things that you must do. If you've got a very important meeting with the director of the chamber of commerce, why take a chance that by becoming involved with another, more immediate problem, you'll miss the appointment? Your natural memory of such things must depend upon your mind's being completely free to remind you ... and you know very well that that won't always be the case.

A good many suggestions for taking care of problems of this nature by means of artificial devices have been fairly well described in Chapter Six, and need not be further discussed here. There are, however, many occasions in life and living when it would be impossible to utilize such devices. And then you must rely solely upon your natural memory to save the day. With a few good, efficient habits, your mind will in time of need be well able to take care of you.

Endeavour to build a pattern of some sort into each series of tasks which you undertake. By regularly following an unchanging order in doing things, you provide your mind with a clear pattern into which it can classify your chores. Thus, the housewife who does the ironing every day immediately after she finishes making the beds enables her mind to refresh her memory of what she's supposed to do next. The bed-making becomes a "cue" to the job of doing the ironing; the ironing will bring to mind the next chore, and so on through the day.

If you've got an important appointment to keep, with the dentist, for instance, your genuine interest in it might be somewhat less than you desire. By resorting to the bonus reward principle, you can increase that interest, in this way: Make the dentist's appointment be only a part of something to remember, by coupling it in your mind with a movie, or dinner at some favourite restaurant. Identify the two things together vividly, as if you always go to see a movie right after an appointment with the dentist. The "package deal" will then seem a lot more inviting to you than did the dentist's appointment alone, and because of increased desirability you'll have a greater chance of remembering it.

Instead of telling yourself, "I must stop in at the office of the gas company and pay my bill", say, "I'm going to see that new comedy at the Such-and-such theatre, right after I stop in at the office of the gas company to pay my bill". Instead of "We've got to spend an evening with that terrible bore Jim", it's "We've going to spend an evening with cute Sally and her terrible bore of a husband Jim."

Vocalization and visualization will often help your natural

memory to recall things. The sound of your own words, the visual scene which will be provided by your imagination, will multiply your chances of remembering—your mind will have that many extra hooks to fish up when the time comes.

If you must tell a friend about something special, and you're afraid that you might not remember when you meet him, visualize the meeting—see yourself walking up to him, shaking his hand and telling him exactly what's on your mind. Recite your part out loud, taking care not to attract too much attention from strangers around you. Listen as you tell him, word-for-word in advance, the information you intend to repeat later. And when you do meet him, your memory will flash back to that pre-meeting imagination and vocalization, reminding you that you've got something special to say.

If there's a big pot-hole in a road that you drive over once in a while, you can increase your chances of remembering it by doing the same kind of thing. When you hit it, say out loud, "That's a very big pot-hole, and it's halfway down Culpepper Street. The odds are that the next time you approach that stretch of road the memory of your last trip will steer you around it.

Vocalization of things will often ease your mind about the fear of not having done things you should have. If you're going on a trip you've probably got a list of things to do before you leave, such as stopping the milk deliveries, making sure that all the water is turned off, and locking the doors. After you've written a note to the milkman, say aloud, "There, the milk is stopped!" As you walk around checking the faucets, announce to the walls, "No water's running here!" On the way out, say to the doors as you lock them, "Now nobody's going to open you!" And when you begin to wonder, as you cross the border line, whether you remembered to stop the faucets, the memory of your speeches will satisfy your anxiety.

To find things that you've put away "in a safe place", it helps if your supply of "safe places" is comparatively small. It also helps if you always put the same things in the same places. And for a "one-shot stash", vocalize the occasion. As you put the Christmas packages in the wine cellar, say aloud, "In you go, Christmas presents, into the wine cellar to hide until Christmas Eve!" You might also visualize the time when you'll retrieve them, seeing a mental picture of yourself creeping up to the wine cellar and throwing open the doors to load your arms with Christmas cheer.

Even without the use of artificial reminders, your memory has plenty up its sleeve. All you've got to do when it comes to remembering things to do, is blaze the trail with vocal and visual signposts, and let your natural memory be your guide.

# A VERY FEW WORDS IN CONCLUSION

SECTION by section, chapter by chapter, you've taken a good look at your memory—first you saw the facets of which it is composed; secondly, its distinguishing characteristics and peculiarities; finally, you read about methods of using your memory most efficiently and profitably for practical remembering.

One special statement was repeated, time and time again, in many different ways and in many different contexts, but it nevertheless emerges as the uniform essence of this book: *Interest grows out of knowledge, and knowledge is best retained through interest.* With a bookful of information about memory under your hat, and with the sure knowledge that *you're going to spend the rest of your life with your own memory*, you should by this time have developed as great an interest in it as anyone could.

By all means your own particular interest in memory will be in its relation to yourself and your life . . . and that's just the most useful kind of interest to have! What you know about memory certainly can't hurt you, but it can't help you either, unless that knowledge has practical application to your own experiences and needs.

By intelligently assigning memory problems to both your natural and your artificial memories, you will be able to save yourself a considerable amount of time and effort. By dispensing with the brute force memorization of things that can be adequately handled by your artificial memory, you will keep your mind clear and well-organized, and ready to tackle any important task. The way you decide to handle each problem will determine the value of the service your memory can impart to you.

Remember, too, that memory is only a way of bringing to mind the things that you already know and understand. No amount of study, repetition, visualization, association or whatever you attempt, will get around the need for understanding. The memory devices about which you've read, in order to be worthwhile, must deal with meaningful material—no monstrous supply of associations will recall a fact that you never knew in the first place.

Memory is no substitution for knowledge, because without the latter, there's no use for the former. So continue to learn, provide your mind with an ever-increasing fund of information, and your memory's service will increase along with it!